CAPITAL CULTURE

First published in 2019 by Aussie Writers
(An imprint of Kirrily King Publishing)
www.aussiewriters.com.au

Cover & Interior Design: David Schembri
Editor: Leanne Manthorpe
Proofreader: Karen Spires

ISBN 9 781876 047221 (print)

ISBN 9 781876 047238 (ebook)

A catalogue record for this book is available from the National Library of Australia

ACKNOWLEDGEMENTS

I would like to thank a few people here who provided support and inspiration for this publishing project I absolutely loved working on. Hayley Weatherburn, John Paynter, Amanda McLeod and Irma Gold, who generously shared their ideas and recommendations. My talented graphic artist, David Schembri, who has worked with me on many exciting projects and has never failed to produce high-quality work, not to mention good humour, which matters most in publishing. I am also grateful to my editor, Leanne Manthorpe, who has been exceptionally talented in her attention to detail, continually demanding the highest quality. Many of the writers commended her talent. Finally, to the authors who have made this volume sing, providing such an eclectic range of high-quality writing and who have also been a pleasure to work with, without exception.

CONTENTS

FROM THE EDITOR

It might be customary to begin with a definition of 'culture', perhaps from the *Macquarie*, as a means of easing into this mercifully short discussion of *Capital Culture*. But I won't do so. While we editors love dictionaries – the more we subscribe to, the happier we are – not all readers do. And my editing university lecturer stressed the importance of the editor acting as advocate for the reader.

More importantly, I don't want to narrow reader expectations of what was a wide authorial brief. The twenty-one talented authors responded to 'Canberra culture' with a gratifyingly heterogeneous collection of short fiction, nonfiction, creative nonfiction and poetry.

Let's imagine this anthology morphs into a mixtape video diary. Fast-forwarding, we see shape-shifting revheads parachuting into Hall Village to drink boutique coffee with Hume and Hovell in front of Blue Poles while keeping an eye out for incontinent canines.

Like all good visuals, this mixtape has a visceral impact. We experience family trauma, the pride of personal achievement, and the isolation of being somewhere we don't quite understand. Loss, hope and humour hit us square-on. We acknowledge inequity, admire resilience, and are comforted by the possibility of redemption. Through all this we hear the rallying cry to celebrate this place, its people and its heritage.

Well, that's how I read it anyway – as I escape murderous office politics to fly over the golden poplars of Lennox Crossing towards the Brindabellas, keen to get home to a bottle of bushfolk shiraz. Readers, have fun compiling your own mixtapes.

Thank you to Suzanne Kiraly (Aussie Writers) for the opportunity to edit *Canberra Culture*. I enjoyed myself and learned a lot about the city I call home.

I am very grateful to the authors for entrusting me with their work; editing is a privilege.

Leanne Manthorpe

INTRODUCTION

In the Australian film, *The Castle*, we are asked to ponder the notion that 'a man's home is his castle', and most of us would agree. But after years of wondering what it is that makes a city feel like home, and grappling with the term 'culture', I am no closer to being able to articulate my feelings for my city.

If you ask people to describe our Australian culture you will get a plethora of responses. Places (icons like the Sydney Opera House, Uluru/Ayers Rock, the Harbour Bridge, the beaches), the cuisine (think lamingtons, meat pies and Vegemite), the native wildlife and landscapes, the vernacular (like the terms 'g'day' and 'barbie' for BBQs), Aussie clothing (think Akubras and green and gold), sport as a national obsession, Aboriginal tourist artefacts and art (think boomerangs), a laissez-faire attitude in our self-deprecating sense of humour which reveals itself in our comedy, and a beer-swilling culture all feature strongly. But we know culture goes much deeper than that. Perhaps *The Castle*'s now famous quote 'it's the vibe of the thing …' comes closest to the heart of our culture than any of the other elements mentioned.

Drilling down deeper, I have always wondered why a city or town feels like 'home'. What makes cities like Canberra, Sydney, Melbourne, Brisbane, Adelaide, Perth, Hobart, and Darwin, or any other town for that matter, unique? Why do we feel at home in our own city and develop a lifelong relationship with it? What do we understand about the vibe of the place we choose to live in?

With more questions than answers, this publishing project was born out of curiosity. I contracted some of our best local writers, chosen for their talent and their love of Canberra and surrounding regions, and asked them to pen a piece that connects with this city. It could be fiction or nonfiction, and not focused on politics, but other than that, there were no stipulations.

Secondly, I ran a writing competition which was launched at the Canberra Writers Festival to reveal fresh writing talent and a more diverse range of voices and opinions. Some of the stories you will find here are from the winners of that competition, truly talented emerging writers from whom you can expect to read much more in the future.

Indeed, my own greatest talent to date, and which has become one of my greatest joys, is to recognise talented writing and to help promote it through the not-for-profit organisation, www.aussiewriters.com.au. This organisation exists purely to identify, inspire, expose and promote talented Australian writers. This project is just one of the many ways we do this.

Sure, Canberra is a common metaphor used too frequently to symbolise the seat of power and politics in this country. But there lives in this city a vibrant culture which also needs to be recognised. And, apparently Lonely Planet recognised Canberra as one of the best places to live in too. (See: https://www.abc.net.au/news/2017-10-25/canberra-named-third-best-travel-city-by-lonelyplanet/9081954.) The local ABC 666 radio station start their breakfast program with acknowledgements to local aboriginal culture, as well as acknowledging listeners calling in to express what they love about living here. I also recall a project which was a survey of the city's population, asking them to identify what they loved about living here, and the result was published on a website with the top one hundred reasons given. It was informative and reinforced my own feelings for our Capital Culture.

This eclectic range of fiction and nonfiction will also help to reveal the complexities of what makes Canberra home to so many who love her. It might just give us a glimpse of the tip of the cultural iceberg that is embedded here and reveal the 'vibe' of the place we affectionately call home.

But the stories also stand alone on merit and entertainment value, so it will appeal to all and sundry, not just residents of this city.

Suzanne Kiraly
Publisher

HAMILTON HUME AND WILLIAM HOVELL WALK INTO A BAR …

CRAIG CORMICK

Hamilton Hume and William Hovell walk into a bar.

Hume, the younger of the two explorers, and far more comfortable approaching a bar than his English-born companion, walks up and asks the bearded man there, 'Can we have some beer?'

'Sorry, we don't serve beer,' the barman tells him.

'You don't?' Hume asks. 'What type of a bar is this then?'

'A coffee bar,' the young man answers.

'A what?'

'Coffee. We have 124 types of coffee. Mostly imported, but two of them, Braddon Blend and Civic Civet, are roasted right here in Canberra.'

'But … but … but you're a barman,' says Hume. 'You must serve beer.'

'I'm a barista,' the other man tells him.

'You look like a bushranger to me,' Hume says.

The barista strokes his long and perfectly waxed beard and says, with an ironic tilt to his eyebrow, 'Are you implying that my beard is as scruffy as your whiskers?'

'What's wrong with my whiskers?' Hume asks him, putting a hand up to feel his long and thick sideburns.

'Well, they don't even look waxed.'

'Do you even know who I am?' Hamilton Hume asks him, slowly turning his head to the side, to show off his best profile.

The barista shrugs.

'Does the name Hume mean anything to you?' Hume asks.

But the barista just shrugs again.

'Like in the Hume Highway,' says Hume, starting to go a little red around the ears now.

William Hovell has joined them now – come up to see what is keeping their beers.

'You might know it as the Hovell trail,' he says.

Hume turns to his companion and frowns. 'I thought we'd discussed that,' he says. But Hovell turns to the barista and says, 'We discovered this place you know.'

'Our cafe?' the barista asks. 'I thought it used to be a used-car yard?'

'No. This whole place.' And he gestures widely around him.

'Braddon?'

'No. The city of Canberra,' Hovell says. 'We came through here in 1824 mapping the land all the way down to Melbourne. I never thought they'd make much of this place though.'

'No, no,' says Hume softly. 'I think if you check our journals and maps we didn't actually come through here. We travelled across a bit further to the north and west.'

'Nonsense,' says Hovell. 'I remember the lake well. I said to you at the time it would be splendid with a few large bridges across it.'

'I think you might be confusing it for Lake George,' says Hume. 'There used to be quite a lake there.'

'Nonsense,' says Hovell again. 'I'm sure we walked through here. The mountains look familiar.'

Hume is about to remind his older companion that he actually got lost whenever they were separated but the barista cuts in, 'So tell me,' he says, leaning in a bit closer now. 'If you had such clear vision for the lake, what were your thoughts on the roundabouts, the Lego block malls and the mishmash of architectural designs of the national monuments?'

Hovell looks to the ceiling, as if searching his memory, and says, 'I seem to recall saying it would make an excellent basis for a miniature model of the city.'

'You wouldn't have been out to Cockington Green this morning by any chance?' the barista asks.

Neither of the two explorers answer.

'And I seem to remember' the barista says, 'the lake here wasn't built until the 1960s. So I don't see how you could have seen it back in the 18-whatevs.'

Hovell interjects quickly, 'We were in Gundaroo yesterday. Now that's a real town. Homesteads. Some shops. A pub that serves beer.'

'We definitely walked through Gundaroo,' says Hume.

'Well it's effectively a suburb of Canberra,' says the barista. 'Even if the Volvos and BMWs have NSW plates.'

'I prefer Yass myself,' says Hume. 'I used to have a homestead there, you know.'

Hovell looks down at his feet as if examining the woodwork there in great detail. He knows how this conversation is going to go unless he changes the topic. How Hume was buried in Yass Cemetery with a nice metal rail around his ornate grave, and he himself was buried in Goulburn, almost in the shadow of its Supermax prison.

But the barista is the first to speak. 'Can't really get a decent coffee in Yass though,' he says.

'But you can get a bloody good beer,' says Hume.

'So I'm guessing two flat whites then?' the barman asks him.

'What's that shiny stuff in your beard?' Hovell asks him.

Just then two spivs in suits come into the coffee bar, talking loudly to each other and simultaneously to people on their phones.

'Graduates!' says the barista, shaking his head. The two suits then start a conversation on the benefits of Ethiopian coffee over Kenyan blends.

'Do you have any Somalian fine-ground beans?' one of them asks.

'Ah, we just brewed up the last of it this morning. Though next week we should have more in.'

The man shakes his head and says, 'They never run out of Somalian in Melbourne.' Then, 'You know what the problem with this city is?'

'Ask these two,' says the barista, nodding to the two explorers. 'They say they're responsible for the city's location and design.'

'Wasn't it Menzies who designed Canberra?' the taller of the two spivs asks. 'Bush capital and all that?'

'No, no, I'm pretty sure it was that Griffin guy,' says the smaller one.

'Who? *Gryffindor*?'

'No. That's Harry Potter. That American architect.'

'Frank Lloyd Wright?'

'I think you might mean Hovell and Hume,' says Hovell helpfully.

'Never heard of them,' says one of the spivs.

'Were they architects?'

'Explorers,' says Hume.

'What were their names again?' asks the small spiv.

'Hume and Hovell,' says Hume.

'That first name sounds familiar,' he says.

'When did you last travel to Melbourne?' Hume asks now.

'Last week in fact. Great coffee in Melbourne did I mention?'

'So you would have driven down the Hume Highway?'

'No. I flew. Who has time to drive to Melbourne?'

'Do you remember that guy who ran the whole way a few years back?' his colleague asks.

'Yes, that was us,' says Hovell.

'No. This guy was really old and wore gumboots. He was a potato farmer or something.'

'He must have been raising money for a charity,' says the other spiv. 'I can't imagine why else you'd go from Sydney to Melbourne on foot.'

'But we did just that,' says Hume. 'And back again.'

'Oh?' says the taller of the two spivs. 'Which charity were you raising money for?'

'We didn't take any charity,' says Hume indignantly. 'We had to raise the money ourselves. We charted the path from Sydney to Melbourne that allowed Canberra to exist. That's what Hovell means when he says we are responsible for this city.'

The two spivs nod their heads and give that sort of vague smile you give when somebody tells you they voted for One Nation. 'Anyway,' says the smaller of the two. 'As I was saying, the problem with this city is that you can't get a decent coffee when you really want one.'

'And it's boring,' says his taller friend.

'And cold.'

'And the suburbs are dull as.'

'And it hasn't got proper trains or beaches.'

'And it has all your bloody politicians,' says a man behind them who has just come into the room and overheard the conversation. He is in his late fifties or maybe early sixties. Is wearing a collared T-shirt and long shorts and has a pair of sunglasses hinged up from his glasses, like they might be surgical implants jutting out from his forehead.

'And where might you be from?' one of the spivs asks him.

'Broken Hill,' the man says.

'Then you need to consider this,' the spiv says. 'They are not actually *our* politicians. They are *your* bloody politicians. They don't come from Canberra. They come from all around the country. From Darwin and Ipswich and Fremantle and Whyalla and Geelong and Broken Hill.'

'And Tasmania,' says the other spiv. 'Don't forget Tasmania or there'll be a ministerial to write.' Then he adds, 'But you have to blame the media too.' And he puts on a newsreader voice: ' "Canberra did this today" or "Canberra decided that today." '

'Like a city can make decisions and do things,' says the taller spiv. 'You don't hear anyone saying, "Broken Hill woke up today, took a look around and went back to sleep." ' They both laugh at that. The man in the shorts does not.

'So I'm looking for a beer,' he says.

'Sorry,' says the barista. 'We're a coffee bar.'

The man looks around suspiciously. 'Looks a lot like a pub to me.'

'Coffee pub,' says Hume.

'Bloody Canberra,' says the old man. 'I remember there was a decent used-car yard here last time I came through.'

Then he starts listing on his fingers. 'There was no Canberra Centre when I was last here, only the Monaro Mall, and Old Parliament House was good enough, and there was a hospital by the lake, and there were two drive-in theatres, and you could get a cold bloody beer at the Civic pub!'

'That would have been in Menzies' time then?' asks one of the spivs.

'And people wore a good safari suit to work,' the man continues. 'No tailor-made guff like you two dickheads are wearing.'

'Are you sure you aren't confusing Canberra with Broken Hill?' one of the spivs asks.

But the old guy's not put off and keeps going, 'I might as well go over to Queanbeyan. I bet they still have decent pubs over there. This city has gone to the dogs. All bloody galleries and apartments and coffee bars. Use to be a bush capital, now it's not much different to bloody Sydney and bloody Melbourne.'

'You're living in the past,' says one of the spivs.

'It's a modern city now,' says the other.

'Good restaurants.'

'Great mountain bike trails.'

'You can buy a good suit.'

'Get a good coffee.'

'Even if they run out of Somalian fine-ground beans sometimes.'

'Close to the snow.'

'No industrial pollution.'

'No mining.'

The old guy screws up his face and says, 'You two dickheads wouldn't know what a decent city was like if it bit you in the arse.'

'Canberra today bit an old bloke on the arse,' says one of the spivs, in his newsreader voice.

'I'm off to Queanbeyan,' the old guy says and storms out slamming the door behind him.

Hume turns to the two besuited spivs and asks, 'Hang on, you two were just criticising Canberra like it was Hovell's navigation skills we were talking about, and now you're defending it?'

'Well,' says the taller of the two, 'rubbishing Canberra is a national sport, and perhaps the only one that unites the nation, but you don't put up with it from somebody who hasn't been here in decades.'

'That's just insulting,' says the other spiv.

'It's like he's from a different era, and criticising this one for being different.'

'Yeah,' says his colleague.

Hume and Hovell say nothing.

'So can we get you two a coffee?' the taller of the spivs asks. 'I recommend the Civic Civet.'

'Ah – I think we'll find our way over to Queanbeyan actually,' Hovell says.

'Better let me lead,' says Hume. 'Or we'll end up in Broken Hill.'

THE SOCIAL CAPITAL

HON DR ANDREW LEIGH MP

Even a century on from its founding, Canberra remains the 'bush capital'. An early description of the region's natural beauty was penned in 1906 by a journalist accompanying the scoping party choosing a capital for the new nation:

> In a district of fine landscapes, Canberra is one of the most picturesque of spots and presented a charming spectacle this morning under the sun from an unclouded sky. It was a clear, frosty morning, such as can be enjoyed at these high altitudes, where a deep breath of the air is like a draft of champagne. Canberra, which lies below Mount Ainslie, and about 200 miles from Sydney, is 2000 feet above sea level … the visitors caught sight from a high ridge of a beautiful panorama – an extensive plain … the white homestead of Duntroon, nestling beneath a hill whose green dome contrasted in a striking degree with the higher and rugged peaks behind, and the rich blue of the mountain ranges still further off, with their tops of snow.[1]

In the century since that passage was written, the decision not to allow development on the mountains that ring the city means that many Canberra residents can look up from a suburban street and see a hill covered in gum trees. It also means that Canberra is a birdwatcher's paradise, with pairs of rosellas and king parrots, not to mention squadrons of cockatoos and galahs. And if you get through spring without being dive-bombed by a magpie, you're doing well.

When Canberra turns on its charm and offers that perfect day where the sun shines, the water glistens and the temperature isn't too cold or too hot, it's easy to see how the city charmed the federal parliamentarians who visited on their tour of potential sites for the new nation's capital. Federal politician King O'Malley once said of the decision about where to site Australia's national capital: 'I want us to have a climate where men can hope. We cannot have hope in hot countries.'[2]

The choice of Canberra was partly luck. Dalgety, a tiny town fifty kilometres south-west of Cooma, was named in the Commonwealth's 1904 *Seat of Government Act* as the location of the new federal parliament. But its chances were dashed by the NSW Parliament, which thought it was too close to Victoria. Then in 1908, a Senate vote between Tumut and Canberra was tied with eighteen votes apiece. It could have gone either way until Anti-Socialist Senator James McColl changed his vote and backed Canberra.

From the outset, Australia looked to the world's best urban planners to design our nation's capital – although King O'Malley's insistence on having the final say led the Royal Institute of British Architects, among others, to suggest to its members that they boycott the competition.[3] A colleague of Frank Lloyd Wright, Walter Burley Griffin heard about the Australian government's competition to design the national capital not long after marrying his wife Marion in 1911. Although it was Walter's name that headed the entry, theirs was very much a collaborative effort. Without Marion Mahony Griffin's elegant drawings, it is unlikely that Walter's design would have grabbed the judges, who chose it over 136 other entries. It is fitting that Walter and Marion are now regarded as co-contributors to the design of Canberra.

Walter Griffin had decided to enter only one international design competition in his career, and the couple gave the Canberra plan their all. As he put it, 'Australia, of most democratic government and bold radical government, may well be expected to look upon her great future, and with it her new Federal Capital, with characteristic big vision.'[4] The Griffins' ideas were ahead of their time. They embraced the new science of town planning and were enthused by the federal government's decision to make the land leasehold, rather than freehold.

The Griffins considered that a city's architecture, landscape and town planning ought to be integrated into a humanised and romantic environment. For a city to flourish, Walter Griffin believed it needed a community with 'the great democratic civic ideal'. As historian David Headon puts it, the Griffins wanted our capital to be a place where citizens enjoyed a high quality of life based on 'egalitarian legislation, genuine public spirit and organic "scientific" cities.'[5] Speaking in Minneapolis in 1912, Walter Griffin told the audience:

> We can all be interested in the Australian Federal Capital city not so much for what it is now or will be necessarily, but because of what it stands for; as an opportunity, the best, I believe, so far afforded for an expression of the democratic civic ideal and for all that means in accessibility, freedom, wealth, comfort, conveniences, scale and splendour.[6]

In 1913, Walter Griffin was appointed as the Director of Design and Construction of the capital and famously drew up the contract himself.[7] The terms placed effective control of the project in Griffin's hands and were humiliating to public officials, in particular to the Secretary of the Department of Home Affairs and the Director-General of Works.

Yet despite the lull in construction that occurred during World War I, the results were superb. Indeed, I can't help wondering whether the Sydney Opera House would have been even closer to its creator's vision if Jørn Utzon had had Walter Griffin's contract negotiating skills.

The city's success has also been due to multiple Prime Ministers. Andrew Fisher long advocated the need for Canberra to have an art collection that befitted a national capital. At the foundation stone ceremony for the National Library, Joseph Lyons said:

> For a young country like Australia, cut off by distance from direct and intimate contact with the progress and thought of older and more experienced nations, there was a greater need for the gathering into the National Library the greatest amount of literature and material possible.[8]

A generation later, Ben Chifley saw the passing of the *Australian National University Act 1946*, establishing the basis for what would become one of Australia's greatest universities. Other Prime Ministers saw different virtues in Canberra. John Curtin liked it because he felt less vulnerable to those pressing special interests upon him.

The Country Party's Earle Page, though only Prime Minister for twenty days, helped Canberra in a very practical way. Faced with a Canberra-bashing federal member from Western Australia, Page induced him to visit for a weekend, whereupon he took the man trout fishing one night (he caught three large ones), hare shooting the next morning, and quail shooting in the afternoon. Henceforth, Page records, the parliamentarian from WA became a Canberra enthusiast.[9]

For Canberrans, the nation's history is our local geography, with suburbs named after the great nation-builders, from Deakin to Chifley, Scullin to Whitlam. On this front, you can't help but feel sorry for Gorton, the only former Prime Minister to make his home in Canberra after retirement. The powers that be decided not to name a suburb after him because of fear that Canberrans would confuse it with the already-gazetted Gordon.

Speaking of names, I can't help pointing out that Canberra is the only Australian capital city named by its Indigenous people rather than the white interlopers. Prior to white settlement, Canberra was best known by the local Indigenous people as the place where they held corroborees and feasted on bogong moths. White settlement began in the 1820s, when Joshua John Moore established a homestead on the Acton peninsula, where the National Museum and the ANU now stand. He called it 'Canberry', which he understood to mean 'meeting place' in the Ngunnawal language.

Canberra continues to evolve as a hub for national conversations, and our meeting places – be they well known, well hidden, salubrious or seditious – are much cherished. One of our great watering holes is Tilley's in Lyneham. Founded as a women's space in 1984, Tilley's originally operated on the rule that men could only enter if accompanied by a woman. The space quickly became popular as a lesbian venue, and one of the city's top live music venues, hosting everyone from Missy Higgins to the Church, Marcia Hines to The

Go-Betweens. Tilley's was named after Matilda 'Tilly' Devine, the Sydney brothel madam who made her money from American servicemen during World War II, and who was known for her utter ruthlessness in dealing with her rivals, including fellow Sydney madam Kate Leigh (no relation of mine, so far as I'm aware).

But the seedy side of life feels far away most of the time in Canberra. Our home is in Hackett, a ten-minute drive from the city centre, and a five-minute walk from the base of Mount Majura. When guests come to visit, we'll often take them straight out for a walk in the bush. Our suburb is designed with walkers in mind, so footpaths conveniently allow us to cut through the streets and make our way up to the bush reserve. If we time it around dusk, the rosellas will swoop over our heads, the kookaburras will be letting out their belly laughs, and the kangaroos will be coming down to the edge of the reserve to graze on the thicker grass.

After seeing the wildlife, we might stroll down to Wilbur's, our local cafe in the Hackett shops, which serves macchiatos and muesli in the morning, before switching in the afternoon to craft beer and gourmet pizza. The cafe was founded by the three sons of James Savoulidis, a Greek entrepreneur who opened the first pizzeria in Canberra in 1966, and taught Zorba's dance to Gough Whitlam. At the time of writing, Wilbur's is being renovated, and the local community is eagerly awaiting its next iteration.

At a time when other Australian cities are choked in traffic, Canberra is comparatively easy to get around. Ours is a city where you don't have to burn a litre of petrol to buy a litre of milk. Corner stores, which have been struggling in many Australian suburbs, are a feature of many Canberra communities. These neighbourhood nodes serve as a focal point for social events. Since Canberra's centenary in 2013, many suburbs now hold annual 'Party at the Shops' events, with sausage sizzles, jumping castles, musical performances and craft stalls.

Canberra has a significant migrant base – not to mention around eighty embassies and high commissions. The largest annual celebration is February's National Multicultural Festival, bringing tens of thousands of people into the city to enjoy food, dancing and music from around the globe. I won't pretend the city is free of racism, but I can't imagine a race riot ever taking place on its streets.

Canberrans wanting to worship can choose from – to name only a few – Anglican, Baptist, Catholic, Evangelical, Lutheran, Pentecostal, Presbyterian, Reformed, and Uniting Churches. You can worship with the Quakers or the Salvation Army, or pray at the Baha'i Centre, the Synagogue, the Mosques, Buddhist temples, Hindu temples, or the Tibetan Buddhist centres. If orthodoxy is more to your liking, there are Coptic, Greek, Russian, Serbian, Macedonian and Ukrainian Orthodox Churches to choose from. Yet I've never heard a murmur from my churchgoing friends about the fact that the local ABC radio station uses the frequency 666, and most people seem quite relaxed about the group of witches that is said to gather on the slopes of Mount Ainslie.

If Canberra was a person, I like to think that it would be an egalitarian patriot, the kind who knows the past, but isn't bound by it. We are proud of the way Australia's history is honoured here in Canberra; in the War Memorial, National Museum of Australia and Museum of Australian Democracy. We were the only jurisdiction to vote for 'Waltzing Matilda' as the National Song in the 1977 plebiscite. We were the only state or territory to vote for a republic in the 1999 referendum. We had the highest percentage vote in favour of same-sex marriage in the 2017 plebiscite.

Walter Griffin believed that he was designing a city for a nation of bold democrats. In an era when Australians are becoming disconnected from one another, Canberra has some of the highest rates of civic engagement in the nation. Canberrans are more generous with our time and money, more engaged in our local community groups, more likely to play sport with our friends and neighbours, and more likely to participate in cultural activities. Canberra is the capital of social capital – a vibrant civic community in the heart of the nation.

1 'The Capital sites: Federal Members' inspection: Canberra and Molonglo: picturesque and well- watered country', *Daily Telegraph*, Tuesday 14 August 1906, p. 7.

2 House of Representatives, *Debates*, 8 Oct 1903, p. 5934.

3 Pegrum, R. *The bush capital: how Australia chose Canberra as its federal capital*, 2nd edn, The Watermark Press, Boorowa, 2008, pp. 134–36.

4 Griffin, WB. 'Canberra: the architectural and developmental possibilities of Australia's capital city', *Building*, Volume 13, 12 November 1913, pp. 65–72.

5 Headon, D. *Canberra: those other Americans*, Canberra: Chief Minister's Dept., 2009, p. 7.

6 'Planning a federal capital city complete: interesting talk on the subject: before the Minneapolis Builders' Exchange, by Walter Burley Griffin.' *The Improvement Bulletin (Minneapolis)*, Vol 55 no. 25, 16 November, 1912, p. 16–17. Griffin's address, of the same title, was delivered to the Minneapolis Builders' Exchange in early November 1912.

7 Harrison, P. 'Griffin, Walter Burley (1876–1937)', *Australian Dictionary of Biography*, Vol 9: 1891– 1939, Gil–Las., Melbourne University Press, 1983. See also *Federal Capital City: agreement between the Minister for Home Affairs and Mr. W. B. Griffin*. Tabled by the Minister in the Senate, 31 October 1913.

8 'National Library: Foundation Stone Ceremony: Distinguished Gathering', *Canberra Times*, 24 November 1924, p. 4.

9 Page, E. *Truant surgeon: the inside story of forty years of Australian political life*, edited by Ann Mozley, Sydney, Angus & Robertson, 1963, pp. 166–67.

TO EASTLAKE AND STABLE

BEN GRAY

It was within a few days of qualifying as a fireman at Goulburn locomotive depot in January 1922 that I first saw Canberra.

The older locomotive drivers at the depot had wished me on my way with such quips as, 'They're a queer mob down in the Federal Capital, Gus,', 'Gonna try your hand at bootlegging?' and, 'Don't worry – the pollies'll kill prohibition if they ever shift from Melbourne.'

I didn't know what to expect, yet I hadn't quite pictured it to look quite so … plain.

The further you got along the 'Federal Territory Railway' from Queanbeyan, the more temporary it felt.

Fewer earthworks.

More track laid straight on top of paddocks.

Fewer fences.

Tracks laid down into an expansive, grassy bowl rimmed by commanding mountains to the south and rolling hills to the north.

It was as if the government financiers and the gangers who built it held a bet each way on whether the city would eventuate. More likely, the financiers didn't want to lose out if the current marriage of government and graziers never quite became a city. It was a gambler's vision befitting of its origin in the home of the race that stops a nation.

The two biggest colonies had had their row, and this was the umpire's call.

This was Canberra.

That unresolved wager was playing in my mind when my driver, Frank, drew the train up at an earthen bank in what stood for the main railway yard at Eastlake (now Kingston). From my side of the engine I looked over to him with an enquiring gaze that proffered the obvious yet unspoken question.

'Yep.' He answered, after a brief acknowledgement of my gaze, sitting back in his seat. His weathered facial features leaned into similarly weathered and dirty hands, cupped to light a cigarette.

We had arrived.

Despite this open expanse being our 'Federal Capital' for more than a decade, the streetscape was still sparse.

The few hotels and government buildings that did exist were placed peculiarly distant from each other. It gave the city the appearance of a model only slightly more lifelike than the one that had won the international competition in 1912 – albeit with a greater abundance of livestock.

'Oi!'

I returned my attention to where Frank was sitting in the driver's seat, now with one leg propped up on the cabin wall.

'You can have a gander around after you've got the fire up. Get on the banjo.'

He pointed to the shovel. With its specially curved sides to prevent the lumps of coal from falling off during the arc from the engine's tender into the firebox, the railway's shovel looked nothing like a banjo. As a junior, you didn't argue.

Best to keep shovelling.

I knew from the other drivers that Frank had been to London and Paris with the AIF during the war and that on a good night back in a Queanbeyan public house, he would regale people with stories of these famous cities. Mid-shovelling, my eyes met those of a solitary cow chewing methodically on a lump of grass behind the railway fence.

I began to understand Frank's disinterest in this excuse for a capital.

The half-dozen passengers who had ridden along to take up their various employments had now left the yard. As there was no permanent passenger station yet in Canberra, railway staff from Queanbeyan rode in with us each day on the engine to administer the contractors in the yard and receipt outwards goods. Their consignment books for outwards goods were always pristine; at that stage the Federal Capital didn't produce anything. Later, when people learned of my stint in the Territory, they would invariably offer the uninvited opinion that it still didn't.

I often saw those staff propped against a tree in the yard in the afternoons, hipflasks and longnecks in hand, sipping as they waited for us to finish up to take them back over the border. This was another odd feature of the Territory – you could bring in as much grog as you liked. You just couldn't buy it here.

My exploration continued after we had dragged a load of coal wagons over a series of empty dirt roads and past the government printing office up to the Power House – a formidable, stocky building, out of place in the pastoral landscape.

As we waited for the plant foreman, I took in the scene beyond the engine to the west, at what looked like the start of a construction site. Timber and building materials were stockpiled around it and surveyor's white marker ribbons lazily fluttered from wooden stakes in the hot January air.

'They were gonna build the real station up there. A mile or so from it,' Frank called over my shoulder, seeing my interest. He pointed further north to a gaggle of low buildings in a paddock. I presumed 'they' meant the Federal Government, still comfortably ensconced in Melbourne at the time. 'It' was the Provisional Parliament House.

I'd heard there was to be a scenic vista from Mount Ainslie to the Parliament House across a lake they'd build later on. I was beginning to become familiar with the phrase. Just about everything here was to be built 'later on'.

'It'll probably stay in Kingston,' I offered.

'Probably,' Frank replied, and, craning his neck to look into the fire, added, 'banjo.'

Best to keep shovelling.

Leaving the Power House, we rode the engine back across the web of sidings and into the main yard at Kingston to collect a load for the north side of the river, for an area known locally as 'Civic Centre'. Another temporary name, I was told.

I jotted down the wagons for the train in my departmental logbook.

'And that one,' Frank added, pointing to a wagon, still covered with a tarpaulin, that we had brought up earlier in the morning from Queanbeyan. I moved to scratch out my previous entry when he nudged the book as if to close it. 'Not now mate. You can chalk it up later.'

We duly added it to the rear of the consist.

After a long draw on the whistle, we tiptoed the engine around a sharp curve and onto the rails leading north, between a cow paddock on one side and a former cow paddock on the other.

Frank noticed me looking over at the Parliament House site as it came into view behind the Power House.

'Madness,' he exclaimed. 'What kind of country doesn't sell grog in their capital?'

'America?' I offered. After all, the whole country was under prohibition.

Frank didn't respond.

I thought he hadn't heard me. I realised it hadn't been a question.

Frank cupped his hand to light another cigarette, trying to ignore the increased vibrations from the rougher track. 'Bring it over the border – no worries. As much as you like.' He took a drag. 'Bloody King O'Malley and his *stagger juice*. I bet they kill it off when they get here.'

We rolled over the paddock on a slightly elevated section of earth known as The Causeway. If Griffin's plans held sway, the line would persist along this alignment through the main part of town to a permanent station and on to Yass.

That would be, as ever, later on.

Clumped around an old homestead to the east was the Royal Military College at Duntroon; another group brought here to fill the place out, with as much of a say about it as the livestock they had displaced.

The brakes squealed as Frank eased us onto a temporary bridge across the Molonglo River. Whereas the rest of the Federal Capital Territory felt new and aspiring, this bridge always felt temporary and unimaginative, and indicative of the thriftiness of the city's construction.

Without a word, we both headed to separate sides of the engine as Frank held the train at the mandatory ten miles an hour, ready to jump if it gave way.

It was a habit borne of little forethought. The drop to the river was a good dozen or more feet below, and the riverbank rose steeply on either side. I'd heard that the few Aboriginal people left in the area steered clear of this section of the river, which was as good a sign as any.

I glanced across at Frank to distract myself, only to find his gaze also fixed on the water.

The bridge released a groan, as if awoken, flexing to hold the train as it crossed.

The rails clanged with each passing of a steel wheel.

More groaning, and that inimitable squeak of timber against timber.

The cacophony mercifully faded as the front wheels edged onto solid ground again.

I rested on the shovel in relief.

Frank was already looking up the line ahead. 'Righto, Gus. Banjo.'

Yes. Best to keep shovelling.

Like the bridge, the ride along the rest of the track felt as if the land was protesting indecision.

Build a line properly or tear this one up.

Get off the fence and pick a side.

It wouldn't be having a bet each way.

The yard at Civic Centre was flanked by more substantial trees and more buildings, feeling altogether a more established, more natural development than on the south side.

As we bounced over the railway crossing and into the yard, Frank drew the train up to a small loading bank next to the line.

There were more people there to meet the train than I had expected. Men in waistcoats without ties, some still wearing canvas aprons to protect finer work clothes. All workers. Bar staff from one of the hotels. They left the load of timber untouched, instead descending on the wagon with the tarpaulin.

I paid them little attention as we cut the engine off the train, yet as Frank drove it back down the other end, I noticed they had backed two lorries up onto the bank.

Frank nosed the engine up to the train and fastened the brakes. We would head back into Eastlake shortly, and I took the opportunity to complete my logbook for both the journey over and the return. It would save me some time when I came to clock off.

A clatter and a lurch of tyres on crunching dirt made me look up. The first of the lorries from the covered wagon had hit a pothole within a few feet of the railway crossing and a crate now lay split on the ground behind its tailgate.

A man from the passenger's side stared down at liquid foaming into a pool around the crate.

He glanced around for onlookers, meeting my gaze. Even at this distance, the bottles of beer poking out from the broken crate were unmistakable.

The lorry driver joined him and briefly looked over at me also, before nudging his helper's shoulder and motioning to lift the crate back into the tray.

I pondered the legality of what had unfolded on the road and noticed Frank had been watching the scene from the locomotive's tender.

He wandered over to me, looking down at the logbook and read the last entry.

Locomotive No 120. Four empty open wagons. To Eastlake and stable.

I felt like he had earned this little victory over the capital. It was a dumb law anyway, and the pollies probably would kill it. Later on.

Frank hopped up onto the driver's seat, gave a long draw on the whistle, and released the air from the train's brakes. 'Banjo, Gus.'

I dropped the logbook into my bag and thrust the banjo into the pile of coal.

Best to keep shovelling.

THE DAY I WAS MISTAKEN FOR A NUDIST

TIM THE YOWIE MAN

'Hey Tim, are there any ocean beaches near Canberra where I can legally swim naked?' audaciously asked an email from 'Celeste' that lobbed into my inbox a few weeks ago.

As someone who prefers a 'togs-on' patch of sand on which to spread my towel, I was somewhat taken aback by the next line of Celeste's request which read, 'Someone told me, you'd be just the man to know!'

After a flurry of subsequent email exchanges, it turns out my curious correspondent confused your Akubra-clad columnist's vocation of a naturalist (one who studies nature) with that of a naturist (basically, another term for a nudist).

Armands Beach near Bermagui is the only legal clothing-optional beach between Nowra and the Victorian border. [Photo: Armands Beach Leisure Group & Sapphire Coast Tourism]

What's more, after a bit of digging, due to similar spelling of the two terms, apparently Celeste isn't the first to make the error. In fact, some nature-based businesses have felt compelled to inform their potential customers of the crucial difference.

The only indication that you about to set foot on a clothing-optional beach is this crudely scratched sign at one of the bush tracks that leads down to Armands Beach. [Photo: Tim the Yowie Man]

Take, for example, Aurora Expeditions who entice nature lovers on adventure cruises to showcase the natural wonders of Antarctica and beyond.

In the Blog section of their website they carefully point out: 'While we're not in the business of judging what people do at home, it's a fair assumption that we will never have an active naturist on board the Polar Pioneer. It's probably a little cold if you know what we mean … however, you'll always find a naturalist on board our small ship expeditions.'

Having absolved Celeste of her inadvertent indiscretion, I was left intrigued by her question. Sure, I recall as a hormone-charged teenager gawking at topless sunbathers at that little cove to the south of Mollymook, but is there anywhere you can legally sunbathe and swim in your birthday suit?

After a series of calls to councils, it turns out that along the entire length of coastline between Nowra and the Victorian border – the stretch of coast we Canberrans like to refer to as the south coast – there's only one official nude beach. Yes, just one: Armands Beach, just south of Bermagui.

Not that it's easy to find. First, it's hidden off the main road and secondly, the beach's official sign has been stolen several times in the last few years. Rumours abound that the sign-pilfering fiend is a local who opposes the clothing-optional status of the beach.

Armands Beach on a sunny summer's day. [Photo: Armands Beach Leisure Group & Sapphire Coast Tourism]

According to a leaflet in the Bermagui Visitor Centre, this secluded surf beach has a long history of attracting naturists and is named after Frenchman Armand Lemmeric, a migrant who established a farm aptly named The Nook in the bushland behind the beach in 1903.

The leaflet reveals that Lemmeric was a farmer with a penchant for swimming au naturel at the beach. Although they were initially private swims, once word spread, he was soon 'joined by other locals who did not own swimming costumes'.

Nudity continued to be commonplace at the beach, peaking in the 1930s when 'nude cricket matches were held'. I guess it's safe to assume there wasn't any ball tampering, for the players wouldn't have had anywhere to hide the sandpaper. Jokes aside, during the late 1960s and early 1970s, Armands Beach was also the love-in camp site for the first flower power commune at a beach location in NSW.

Armand Lemmeric, a naturist, after whom Armands Beach is named. [Photo: Bermagui Museum]

However, there are no sign of bats 'n' balls, nor hippies with hibiscus flowers protruding from their dreadlocks on the day I recently visited the beach, just an athletic-looking twenty-something local lass rocking the latest neck-to-ankle gym gear, energetically leading her pet poodle up the bush path from the beach. She couldn't have more clothes on if she tried.

Feeling a need to explain why I'm wielding a camera (frowned upon at most nude beaches), I explain that I'm checking out the beach firsthand for my column, and ask her thoughts on its clothing-optional status.

A recent arrival to the area, my friendly dog walker reveals she 'is fine with naturists using the beach'.

'At first I was worried that my puppy would jump up and bite someone's bits,' she laughs, 'but usually there isn't anyone else at the beach, unless it's a hot weekend.'

And today is no different, down on the sand there's no-one else within cooee. All I find baking in the sun are clumps of seaweed strewn across the high tide mark.

Nudity at the beach peaked in the 1930s when 'nude cricket matches were held'. [Photo: Armands Beach Leisure Group & Sapphire Coast Tourism]

Keen to find out more of the beach's colourful past, I perch myself on a rock at the northern end of the beach and call Errol Masterson – he's been swimming here in the raw since 1952.

Masterson reveals he is especially enamoured by the beach's beauty: '... its sapphire-coloured shore break, its rockpools and its lagoon which hold back a freshwater creek.'

'According to local legend, during World War II, Japanese submarines would surface in Armands Bay and come ashore for freshwater,' reveals Masterson. No word on whether they were clothed or not.

Masterson even remembers the day in the 1970s when the beach was completely stripped (no pun intended) entirely of sand following big storms. 'There wasn't a grain of sand left,' he recalls. 'You could hardly recognise it as beach.'

After attracting naturists for the best part of a century, when the Bega Valley Shire Council legalised the beach's clothing-optional status on November 17, 1993, Masterton promptly set up the Armands Beach Leisure Group.

'We're not a club or anything, just a bunch of people who regularly meet at the beach,' he explains. 'Oh, and we also organise Fun in the Sun days to showcase our patch of sand to the wider community.'

For those nervous about visiting Armands for the first time, Masterson has some advice. 'It's a clothing-optional beach, not a nude-only beach, so you can still come in your togs just like any normal beach.'

With no-one around, I'm tempted to get my gear off to see if bathing in the buff really is all it's made out to be, but I quickly chicken out after noticing the length of the pincers on the crabs frolicking in the rock pools at my feet.

While clambering back up the stairs from the beach to my car, a white-bellied sea eagle swooping low over the rainforest canopy sends a goanna slithering through the underbrush. This really is a nature lover's paradise.

Maybe a naturist and naturalist go hand in hand after all.

FACT FILE

Armands Beach: This clothing-optional family-friendly beach is located near the end of Kullaroo Road, about 10 km south of Bermagui. Please note: nudity is limited to the extent of the sands of the beach. The Armands Beach Leisure Group's 'Fun in the Sun Day' is usually held on the second Sunday in March. All welcome. www.armands.org.au

Window into the past: To discover more about Armand Lemmeric and other colourful characters from Bermagui's past, including Zane Grey (a prolific American adventure author who holidayed often on the south coast), pop into the Bermagui Museum (behind the Visitor Information Centre on Bunga St) Friday and Saturday, 10 am–2 pm.

Naturist nooks: There are several 'unofficial' clothing-optional beaches on the south coast, including Moon Bay (yes, that's its real name) in Mimosa Rocks National Park and Keef's Pinch, Eden (although if you are after privacy, beware, as the salmon fishers drone over this bay quite frequently).

Lisa Bray of Canberra takes a cheeky selfie at the Myrtle Beach sign. [Photo: Lisa Bray]

Further north, at Myrtle Beach in Murramarang National Park, the Batemans Bay District and Visitors Nudist Group hosts a 'Natural Day in the Sun'. Meanwhile at Jervis Bay, the small unnamed beach between Nelsons and Blenheim on the White Sands Walk near Vincentia is a regular haunt for those seeking that all-over tan.

Closer to home: If fresh water is more your style, a section of the Murrumbidgee River near Kambah Pool was designated as a nude bathing area under the *Nudity Act 1976*, prior to self-government.

Originally published in *The Canberra Times*, 1 December 2018, and updated for this anthology.

CANBERRA BY NIGHT

SIMON BRYANT

Ahh, Canberra. Much-maligned, much-denigrated, much-ridiculed Canberra.

Canberra, the seat of government and therefore, in the eyes of so many, a city somehow responsible for every unfeeling, short-sighted and wasteful decision ever made by any politician.

Canberra, the home of the Australian Public Service, and therefore entirely populated by cosseted, out-of-touch bureaucrats, more interested in maximising their ludicrously inflated superannuation balances than in serving the interests of hardworking, long-suffering punters out there in the real Australia.

But most damning of all scathing epithets, Canberra the boring. Where dull suburbia rules and nothing ever happens; where domestic thrills are measured in children's sporting trophies; and, where its citizens get their real pleasure only from fleeing the confines of the Territory – to the snow in winter, and around Pooh Corner and over the Clyde to the coast in summer.

Well friend, like you, I held those stereotypes about our national capital, at least until I was subject to, early in the new year, a reluctant twelve-month Canberra secondment in a certain federal department. But then – as I began to enjoy the endless sunshine of Canberra's balmy autumn, the permanently sparse traffic on its magnificently engineered roads, its plethora of brilliant eateries – then my Canberra assumptions and prejudices began to dissipate.

But in late May, one unforgettable weekend shattered my most enduring illusion, my lingering perception that Canberrans lived safe, predictable, boring lives, shielded from the wicked pleasures that abound in the wilds of Melbourne and Sydney.

The scene: Friday, six-thirty, after-work drinks in the branch head's office, and the regular clique of hardened hangers-on had dispersed earlier than usual in response to the siren call of a Raiders' home game. Having no interest in the inevitable disappointment that I already knew lay there, I lingered – in large part too because I was quietly savouring the third glass of an excellent Clonakilla Shiraz, proffered from the branch head's stash, before she too dashed off; not to the Raiders, but to the more cultured milieu of an Albert Hall concert.

Before I knew it, I was alone with just one other, an EL1 who, for the necessary requirements of anonymity, we shall simply call Kevin. A quietish, fortyish, steady sort of fellow, whom I had barely spoken to, or even noticed, in my four months in the office. My chief exposure to him had been at a departmental trivia night some few weeks previously, where his dogged intensity and encyclopedic knowledge of the most arcane trivia had me pigeonholing him as that creature to be avoided at all costs – the office bore. So now, with little prospect of interesting conversation, I briefly contemplated making my escape. But the sacrilege of leaving three-quarters of a glass of Clonakilla stood in my way. Instead, I took another decent sip, and asked Kevin how his week had been.

'Oh, not so bad,' he replied pleasantly. 'Though the Estimates briefings are proving a bit of a handful.'

'Yeah, tough time of year,' I murmured, grimacing in sympathy then lapsing into silence. I reached for the glass, thinking to drain it as quickly as possible and get out of there.

'But I must say I'm looking forward to the weekend. It should be very exciting.'

The surprisingly enthusiastic tone in his voice made me look up from contemplating the bottom of my glass. Kevin was looking directly at me, an odd intensity in his eyes.

'Really?' I responded politely. 'Anything particular in mind?'

Kevin's eyes did not leave mine. 'Well, yes,' he replied, and his voice dropped to a conspiratorial whisper. 'Carol and I have been planning something for a while now. And this weekend looks to be the one to give it a try.'

I had briefly met Carol (again, not her real name) at the trivia night. The impression that lingered was of a short, round woman, with a determinedly enthusiastic approach, to everyone and everything.

'Jolly good,' I replied, trying to avoid his gaze. 'What do you have in mind?'

Kevin continued to stare, distractedly stroking his neatly trimmed beard. He appeared to be struggling with a decision of some sort. His eyes darted around the room briefly, but then fixed on me again. A nervous, slightly embarrassed grin appeared.

'Well, to be honest, Tom, it's not something that Carol and I like to share with other people.' And after a further hesitation, 'Unless we think they're open to new experiences. And Carol thinks that you would be.'

Some rather disturbing images began to crystallise in my mind, all featuring me, Kevin and the enthusiastic Carol.

'Oh, I'm not sure she's right about that,' I protested. 'After all, she's only met me once.'

'Oh, Carol is an excellent judge of character,' Kevin insisted. 'And believe me, she was very taken with you. Very taken.'

The lure of the wine was now completely replaced by an urgent need to get out of there as quickly as was humanly possible. I rose to my feet, but Kevin beat me to it.

'We would love you to join us,' he persisted. 'We've got it planned for tomorrow night.'

'Sorry about that,' I stammered, 'but I'm afraid I've got something on tomorrow night.'

'That's a pity,' Kevin replied, his disappointment palpable. 'A real pity. The Brindabellas are wonderful by night at this time of year.'

'Sorry? The Brindabellas?'

'Yes, particularly by moonlight. Perfect for spotting them.'

'Them?' The conversation was veering in an entirely unexpected direction. I wasn't sure whether to be relieved or further alarmed.

Again, Kevin looked a tad embarrassed. But he had clearly resolved to take me into his confidence.

'Yowies.'

'Yowies?'

Yes, yowies. They're hairy, humanoid creatures who ...'

'I know what yowies are, Kevin. But what makes you think they're in the Brindabellas?'

'I'm confident, Tom, very confident. We've done the research, you know. And we've gathered hard evidence. Not enough for the doubters, of course. Most people have closed minds. Wouldn't believe us, no matter what.'

I looked at Kevin. At his earnest, trusting gaze. Almost pleading with me to accept him, and his crazy proposition, as credible. Suddenly, I felt a surge of sympathy for him, and for his pleasant little wife who no doubt loyally supported his wacky obsession. If this was the only way they could get some excitement into their mundane lives, who was I to shatter their illusions? And what the heck, in reality I had nothing on the next night and perhaps a moonlit drive to the Brindabellas might be a bit of a lark.

*

We reached our destination, a fire trail somewhere along the Mount Franklin road, past Piccadilly Circus, around 11 pm. Carol and I in the back seat of the Subaru Outback, Kevin driving, with his box of yowie-spotting equipment strapped securely into the front passenger seat. The large aluminium container looked perfectly sturdy to me. I had suggested it could have been quite safely stowed in the boot, but

Kevin was insistent: 'Believe me, Tom, there's some very sensitive gear in there. Motion sensors, expensive flashes, tape recorders ... I like to keep an eye on them over these rough tracks.'

Fair enough, but it meant for the entire journey I was subject to Carol's patter, as she burbled blithely on about the overwhelming evidence of yowies up here in the Brindies. Giant footprints (admittedly rather poorly defined), strange hairs found in their sticky traps, recordings of unearthly roars and screams ... all of it was interesting, if not entirely convincing. Indeed, by the time we pulled up and stepped out into the moonlight, I was actually feeling a frisson of excitement and anticipation.

But that feeling soon dissipated, replaced by an entirely more mundane sensation: extreme, numbing cold. I had forgotten that a clear, still May night in Canberra would inevitably mean a deep frost. And up here in the mountains, the chill was even more extreme. Probably only about minus five, but it felt like minus fifty.

The pain was marginally held at bay while, clad in camouflage gear, we lugged the heavy box down the fire trail and into a secluded valley clearing where, Kevin confidently informed me, yowies were reliably known to congregate. Another half-hour to set up cameras and recorders in various positions, before we settled down in the bushes, under some sort of plastic camouflage cover, to await the hairy visitors.

Despite the close proximity of our bodies, the icy cold quickly permeated everything. Within ten minutes, I was losing the feeling in my extremities, and my head was aching. I found myself fervently hoping either for the yowies to make their appearance, or for sanity to return to my companions. Neither happened, and time dragged on.

'Bit cold, isn't it?' I whispered eventually, through chattering teeth.

'Shhhh!' they chorused. I lapsed back into stricken silence and tried to think warming thoughts – of open fires, hot pizzas and the like. It didn't work.

Another half-hour of this torture, and I sensed that even my stoic companions were starting to flag. I was about to suggest perhaps we should give it away for the night, when I felt Carol stiffen beside me. She leaned forward and peered more intently through her spy-hole in the cover.

'What is it?' I whispered.

'Shhhh!' they hissed.

Then I heard it. The unmistakable sound of someone, or something, approaching. And something very large too, from the magnitude of its footfall and the noise of twigs snapping and leaves rustling as it made its way towards us.

Then, in the still night air, a loud, unearthly cry; part-squeal, part-grunt, and frighteningly close at hand.

'Oh my God!' cried Carol, involuntarily seizing my arm.

'Shh!' whispered Kevin, still focused on the task at hand.

Then suddenly, the bushes in front of us parted and it was on us! Flashes blazed, cameras clicked. The clearing before us turned briefly from night to day. To reveal the largest pig I had ever seen, standing there snorting and grunting, its breath steaming in the frigid air, its eyes reflecting red in the glare of the flashlights as it stared suspiciously at our flimsy cover.

'Oh my God!' cried Carol again, and her grip tightened on my arm.

'Shit!' said Kevin. And, as if to emphasise his descent into the vernacular, 'Bugger, bugger, bugger!' Then he stood, flipped away the cover, and strode into the clearing.

'Clear off, you big, useless thing! You've ruined our night.'

The feral pig stared at him briefly, then obediently wheeled around and trotted away down the path. I too stared at Kevin. He was either incredibly brave, or even crazier that I had previously thought.

'Well, that's it, I suppose,' said Kevin. 'We'd better pack up. They won't be coming through now. We'll just have to wait until next full moon.'

*

Kevin and Carol seemed in good spirits as we bounced along the rough metal road, back to civilisation. The failure of tonight's mission was clearly only a temporary setback. For my part, I was solely focused on regaining the feeling in my limbs, and just hoping that frostbite had not set in. My teeth were still chattering uncontrollably.

Then I noticed that Carol had produced a thermos from somewhere. She leaned towards me.

'Would you like a hot cocoa?' she inquired solicitously. 'You still seem a bit cold.'

'Oh, yes please,' was my fervent reply. 'That would be wonderful!'

I could feel the heat from the steaming liquid as she poured it from the flask and leaned across in the dark to hand the cup to me. But just as she did, the car hit a particularly large pothole and bounced alarmingly. I felt Carol's hand seize my knee as she steadied herself, then handed me the cocoa.

'Thank you,' I said. 'You're a lifesaver.'

Carol stayed leaning in towards me, her hand still on my knee. 'You poor dear,' she whispered. 'That'll warm you up on the inside. Now let me warm you on the outside.' And her hand began to move in ever-widening circles.

'Sorry about the rough ride!' yelled Kevin from the front. 'You two all right back there? Getting on okay?'

'Oh, we're getting on just fine, dear,' said Carol cheerfully, her hand moving inexorably upwards from my knee.

FRINGE FOLK

JENNY MORRIS

On the map of New South Wales
there sits a strange outline
a sort of bird-like elephant
a hard shape to define.
A Territory within a State
it's called the ACT
with Canberra as its beating heart
bush capital city.
Who lives outside this quirky sketch
this oddly surveyed scrawl
that's squiggled on a map of Aus
beyond an urban sprawl?
It is the home of Fringe Folk
who chose to cross this line
to settle on an acreage
thinking the line benign.

*

Most Fringe Folk were suburbanites
not born of farming stock
they dreamed of rustic ventures
so bought a rural block.
They thought themselves *Canberrans*
escaping the rat race
to pursue endeavours for
which they needed space.
Obviously so innocent
of what this would entail
thought Canberra was there for them
and that they could avail
themselves of all its services
like schools police and health.
This friendly close proximity
would share its common wealth.

*

These bush folk thought that years of toil
within the ACT
and doing all their business there
would surely guarantee
them access to these services
and fatten Canberra's purse
with reciprocal cash payments
that their State would reimburse.
These poor misguided bush folk thought
this would then erase
the avian-like pachyderm
but this is not the case.

*

Seemingly there's not enough
  that's returned by their State
to balance Canberra's budget
  and so expunge the slate.
The critter guards its border
  is vocal in defence
it tweets and trumpets loudly
  yes capital offence!
The rim folk caught betwixt between
  are slipping through the cracks
they find they are invisible
  despite their paying tax
in trust that the ACT
  and State of New South Wales
acknowledge their disparities
  and make sure sense prevails.

*

So is it only Fringe Folk
  who cross from side to side?
No! City goes to country
  across this great divide.
The Fringe Folk are so sick and tired
  find hard to disregard
the Canberra trucks filled up with waste
  that's dumped in their backyard.
A backyard that grows beef and lamb
  and olives for their oil
nuts eggs and fruit and vegetables
  on land with fragile soil.

And famous are the vineyards
  that make cool climate wine
that Canberra likes to call its own
  though they're across the line.
Then off to farmers' markets
  for all of us to savour
the produce with few food miles
  so fresh and full of flavour.

*

Taught salutary lesson once
  we had to both liaise
when devastating bushfire set
  scrub and house ablaze.
For grasslands blur the border
  merge Territory with State
and fires will rage both back and forth
  they'll not discriminate.
Either side a fire's a fire
  the line is burned aside
no demarcation on a map
  fire sees no marked divide.

*

Perhaps we're only stale mates?
I'd argue that's not so
we're not too close for comfort
insisting quid pro quo.
The line's schismatic incline
implies we are divided
but we are all *Canberrans*
with needs that aren't one sided.
Our cartographic closeness
should be of fundamental
benefit to all of us
and not be detrimental
to frank and friendly discourse.
Ignore the politics
stir give and take with compromise
into the region's mix.

*

All for one and one for all
is apropos advice.
This lineation on a map
should not come at a price.
To bring about consensus
discard the *yours* and *mine*
we need to meld our border.
Don't let the line define.

2017

GIRL TRANSPORTED

IRMA GOLD

'Abby, wake up.' Fran's voice is a hiss against her ear.

'What?' Abby slurs, her body sleep-filled.

'Get *up*. *Now*.'

Abby pulls herself to sitting, brushing away dreams. From outside comes gentle clanking, the shuffle of chains. 'Where're we going?'

'Just get in the car.'

The makeshift bed spills Abby into the night. The sky is milky with moon and cloud. It turns her nightie transparent. Even in the masked light Abby can see that Fran's eye is purple, a split grape.

Her brother has already moved Mick's car into position. He is attaching the weight distribution bars. 'Quick,' Dan says. The whites of his eyes are glowing.

Abby climbs in the back, rubs at her goosepimply arms. The sandpapery sound of it fills the small space. Dan throws himself into the front seat and Fran turns the key in the ignition. The noise leaps into the night like an alarm; now things are coming into focus. Abby imagines Mick's face rearing up against her window.

They move slowly through the caravan park. Abby wishes Fran would put her foot to the floor, but instead they creep over speed humps and attempt to slide snake-like from the place. The problem is Mick's caravan. Even at this pace it jostles against them, resisting abduction.

But soon they are out. Fran winds her window down all the way and sticks her whole head out into the force of the gushing air. She shouts, as if trying to break her lungs, 'Yeeeeee*ha*!' Beside her Dan has a wide-angled smile. The car weaves about and the caravan jounces dangerously behind them. Abby grips at the seat as if it holds brakes.

By morning they are nudging the northern edges of Canberra. On Northbourne Avenue they run straight into Summernats traffic. People are camped out along the central nature strip, either side of the road. A rabble of tents and camping chairs and eskies. Cars rev past, showing off, leaving behind screens of smoke. Girls wearing only bikini tops and ripped shorts cheer. Fran forgets that they are supposed to be chasing up an old mate of hers, finding a place to set up, and instead they deposit the caravan across from Exhibition Park.

Fran's driving has caused a hurricane and they rummage for clean clothes. Abby finds her shorts on top of the microwave. Fran plasters concealer around her eye but it only makes the damage more obvious. When she puts on mascara she winces.

'Let's go, you two,' she says. 'Can't believe we got so freakin' lucky!'

They tumble into the hot day to buy tickets. As they wait in line the throaty roar of cars is a lure. The wind pushes an empty UDL can into Abby's foot. She watches as Fran hands over a week's worth of money.

The place smells of fumes and sunscreen and testosterone. Men prance about topless, T-shirts hanging limply from back pockets, tatts on display. Even though it is early in the day the booze is flowing. Fran buys a beer for her, one for Dan. 'This is my kind of place,' she grins.

Cars the colours of Skittles try to outdo each other on the cruise route. Abby thinks they look stupid revving their guts out at ten kays an hour. Some of the utes have couches in the back loaded up with girls. One has its rear bumper so close to the ground even a teensy ripple in the asphalt would be its undoing. Abby can't see the appeal, but Dan is feverish with excitement.

One man with a KFC bucket for a hat jumps out of the crowd and onto the cruise way with a mock road sign instructing, Show Us Ya Tits. The crowd starts chanting, Tops Off! Tops Off!

'Woohoooo,' Fran screams and pulls her singlet up over her face with one hand, spilling beer in her hair and exposing a grubby once-white sports bra. With the other hand she pulls a bra cup down. A boy near them who can't be more than sixteen points at her, 'Shit yeah.' Abby slinks further back into the crowd.

They watch a burnout comp. Smoke streams from the cars like water, their engines pushed so hard the sound cracks. The smell of burning rubber is raw, intoxicating. Against her will Abby is mesmerised. There is skill here, and the adrenaline is infectious. A lemon car disappears inside a tornado of smoke, slithers of tyre are flung from it. When it re-emerges its driver is pumping his fist through the open window, pumping the crowd up. 'He's molesting the track!' a commentator cries. 'This car is totally mental. Built purely for skids.' A chubby man standing against the rail next to Abby says to his mate, 'Fark, what a beast.' The mate sucks on a tinny. He is wearing red Y-fronts over the top of his shorts with the slogan, I'm proud of my tool.

When the car narrowly misses crashing into the barrier closest to them, Abby turns to Fran and discovers that she has disappeared. Dan too. There is no point going to the Information tent; Fran won't be looking for her. The noise is giving Abby a headache so she escapes to the pavilion, wanders around looking at hose fittings and car jewellery and super shiny rims. The press of so many people starts to grate. She sits in a toilet cubicle. It is an outside concrete block, unlit and cool. In the semi-dark with the engines only a backdrop of noise, there is calm. A mosquito drifts up from somewhere, its legs zebra-striped. It weaves towards Abby's face and she lunges at it, her hands clapping down on air. She hurriedly pulls her undies and shorts up in one swift movement, and stumbles back outside. From a tap low on the wall she drinks water in great gusting gulps.

She walks and walks, laps the grounds twice, hoping to spot Fran, or Dan. She half-heartedly watches the Miss Summernats competition for a while. 'Let's hear it for Suzette,' the bloke with the microphone says. 'She's a Summernats virgin, so give it up. Don't be shy.'

Suzette blows a kiss to the crowd, walks awkwardly across the stage in her ridiculously high heels.

'So what would make you a good Miss Summernats?' a woman in a black pantsuit asks in imitation of an interview.

'Because I'm guaranteed to *rev* you up,' she cries, and turns to wiggle her bum at the crowd.

'All the girls are stunning this year, really raising the bar,' Microphone Man says through the catcalls.

'Sure are, Waz,' Pantsuit agrees. 'Absolutely of a high quality this year so it's gonna be tough.'

The day is starting to disappear. Bugs are flying at the lamps on stage, probably biting at the girls' legs. Abby's stomach roils with emptiness. On a bench there is a paper cup with some leftover chips, and she edges her way over to it. When she hopes no-one is looking she pulls it quickly onto her lap, shoves the limp things into her mouth. They are cold and taste only of oil, but they fill her up.

She tosses the cup in the bin and starts walking again. Still no sign of Fran. A knot of men are loitering on the path, empty cans lined up along the wall beside them. 'Oi, wanna root?' one of them yells at her, prompting raucous laughter. Abby pretends not to notice, passes without making eye contact. 'What are ya, a lezzo?' he shouts. More laughter.

When they are well behind her, Abby runs. Past the cars still bouncing on the cruise strip, out the front gates, past the free shuttle bus ferrying horny, sun-addled men to a Mitchell brothel, and on towards the car park. When she finds Mick's caravan she drops to the dusty ground, and crawls under it. Lying on her back, the guts of the van close to her face, she waits.

GHOSTS OF CANBERRA

MARION HALLIGAN

Canberra has acquired plenty of ghosts in its little more than a hundred years of existence. Turn your head just a bit sideways, squint a little, and above all look with the mind's eye, and you will see this shadowy population.

Go to Old Parliament House, for instance, and you may observe the tall heartbroken figure of Gough Whitlam, intoning 'Well may we say "God save the Queen", because nothing will save the Governor-General.' He was right, too, for Kerr is hardly even a ghostly presence on the vice-regal scene he became so badly. Although perhaps there is a faint shade at the Melbourne Cup, where he gave a rambling drunken speech, dressed so prettily in his pearl grey tailcoat and, surely, his top hat.

Then there's Mr Menzies, gazing misty-eyed at the young queen. 'I did but see her passing by,' he nearly sings. Or the past self of Paul Keating, to the horror of monarchists everywhere, actually touching her. Mal Meninga, planning to stand for local parliament, rushing out of the radio studio and the interview that was to begin his career and in fact ended it. It was embarrassing and funny and somehow admirable. Malcolm Fraser with his razor gang and his claim that life wasn't meant to be easy.

A careful observer sees public ghosts and personal ones, ones that belong to the city and indeed the country, and others to just an individual or two.

There is the bricklayer who came from Italy and worked on a number of important buildings. He'd drive his family round the city and point them out. *I laid the bricks in that building. In that building, in that one* … his daughter remembers him saying.

Many Canberra buildings are now public ghosts. I think with regret of Glebe House, original rectory to the Church of St John the Baptist. It stood in the present Glebe Park, which is a sad remnant of the considerable acreage the rectory once possessed. It's hard to believe that a city as new as Canberra would demolish a fine old house, Georgian in style if not quite in date. I suppose we should consider ourselves lucky they didn't knock down the church while they were at it. Apparently the bricks were used to build the Queanbeyan–Acton Football Club at Manuka. What stories they could tell.

The Capitol Theatre at Manuka went, to be replaced by a cinema complex with two screens. Useful, I suppose, but the old building was rather nice Art Deco. In the 1980s we lost the Town House Motel, with its Clement Meadmore ironwork (happily, two panels are on display in the NGA's Sculpture Garden) and its restaurant in the shape of an ark, called Noah's, which gave its name to a chain of hotels. The Town House was designed by Enrico Taglietti, and his work has not been preserved as it might have been. The Dickson library flourishes, but I mourn the loss of Taglietti's Center Cinema in Civic which showed interesting films for almost thirty-seven years. It closed down (screening *Doctor Zhivago*, the film it had opened with) and turned into a nightclub. The architect said he'd rather it was blown up.

Canberra hasn't done well with traditional pubs. The city was never a place for pubs on corners, as in English towns and old cities like Newcastle or Melbourne, so people could wander down for a pint and not have to take a car. Most that it had it's got rid of. Whatever happened to the Dickson pub? Or the pub in Narrabundah? Such fine buildings. Both Tagliettis. And of course the Civic, which was a good old city pub. Now the bus interchange sits where drinkers once spilled out of the Civic's public entrance on Alinga Street.

Town planners often fail to take into account people's affection for their built environment, which doesn't always have a lot to do with its beauty, but the ways in which it belongs to the people who use it or dwell in it.

Probably the angriest ghost is the Royal Canberra Hospital. Not architecturally attractive like the work of Taglietti, but a place dear to people's hearts; where they were born, or their children were. Griffin had put it on his original plan. It was beautifully situated on the lake at Acton Peninsula, not to mention near the ANU, handy for a future medical school. And it was supposed to be able to keep in step with future needs.

It was decided to consolidate public hospital services at Woden Valley Hospital (which, now, as Canberra Hospital, has consequently become pointlessly large with parking that is a nightmare – if you are not already sick you become so). The Royal Canberra Hospital site would become the National Museum of Australia. As long-time local doctor Marcus Faunce said, '… many Canberra citizens were either bewildered, angered or saddened …'

There were a lot of buildings on the site and it was decided to blow them up. The plan was to use a natty technique of causing them to implode, so they would collapse neatly into themselves. In July 1997, encouraged by the ACT Government, some 100 000 people came to see the spectacle. They brought picnics and rugs and watched from the park across the lake. They weren't happy with the hospital's destruction, but maybe they wanted to say goodbye.

The implosion was a failure. The building didn't disintegrate properly and would have to be manually demolished later on. The explosion was not contained and debris went whizzing across the lake. Tragically, a large chunk of metal killed a twelve-year-old girl, and nine people were injured. The death of the little girl Katie became a focus for people's anger at the loss of the hospital.

The demolitions are still happening. As I write this, various blocks of flats are being knocked down, some to make way for the new light rail, others because in theory they are past their use-by date, others because this new transport route needs glossier dwelling places to line it. But less this, I think, than that they were public housing, neglected by the mostly unhappy people who lived there. I remember when I was first married and the flats were fairly new, I'd have loved to live in one of these neatly designed buildings right on the edge of Civic. I thought it would feel very European. Instead, most new Canberrans were forced by horrendous rents to buy a house, mortgages being cheaper because of large government subsidies on rents for public servants obliged to live here.

I'm not sure why these blocks of public housing, which were well-designed, pleasant and close to amenities, didn't work. As well as the ghosts of their absences, they will also leave behind the shadows of the good things that might have been.

People, buildings; finally trees.

Canberra may be known as the bush capital, but it is also the largest urban forest in the world. For some time I was cross with what I thought was failure to water during the last drought, when a lot of our trees died. But this is neglect, and more understandable than outright destruction. I am heartbroken by the wanton chopping down of trees, for instance for the construction of road intersections at Pialligo. Doubtless the perpetrators would argue that it was necessary; I don't think so. The roads should have taken another path.

I think fondly of the glorious poplars that were sacrificed to Lake Burley Griffin some fifty years ago. When it was still the Molonglo River, the future lake had crossings instead of bridges, low causeways scarcely above water level. One of these was called Lennox Crossing and ran from behind the Hyatt Hotel to below the hospital at Acton. Lennox Gardens recalls this. The crossing was surrounded by magnificent great poplars that turned marvellous gold in autumn. When I was teaching at the old Canberra High and we lived in Red Hill (in a converted garage, no flats available, houses too dear to rent), my husband used to drive me along this route, going very fast because we were always late. So beautiful, in all seasons of the year.

The poplars went when the Molonglo was dammed. Inevitable, of course, you can't make water detour round beautiful trees. But I still feel sad about it.

And now, the long destructive tentacles of the light rail again. Northbourne Avenue completely denuded. Such a glorious entry to the city it was. Think how many cities have hideous industrial areas that have to be traversed before you get to their beauties, but Canberra reached out and spoke to you from the moment you approached. Yes, I know the light rail is supposed to be a good idea (even better when there's one to Belconnen, and the airport, and Tuggeranong). Yes, I know it was in Griffin's plan. Yes, I know they are going to replant the avenue – I do believe replacement trees are cheerfully growing in their pots in the nursery – yet still I mourn these lost trees. They will haunt their devastated home for a long time to come.

THE LAST TEA LADY

BRIAN FRANKLIN

The public service of the 1970s was a far different animal to that of today. Cafe latte had not been invented and the rattle of the tea trolley was a familiar sound signalling fifteen-minute morning and afternoon breaks in the working day.

At that time I was employed in the Property Division of the Department of the Interior. This mega-department managed the ACT as well as national assets. My particular interest was land management, acquisitions and disposals. We were located in Electricity House at 222 London Circuit, then the headquarters of ACTEA, ACTEW's predecessor. The departmental offices on the eighth floor overlooked the changing panorama of our developing city.

As was the practice with all Tea Ladies, ours was a character of considerable note and a tour de force of her profession. A woman of substantial proportions and forceful European consonants, Mrs J executed her responsibilities with efficiency and good humour. If you were really in favour, tea was delivered to your desk; if not, there could be an interminable wait for corridor service.

Mrs J came to formal departmental notice in the campaign period prior to the 1972 election when she proudly plastered a 'Vote Labor' sticker across the hot water urn on the tea trolley. A staff member from Personnel was instructed by senior management to rectify the situation – certainly no-one would have volunteered for such a risky task. Approaching Mrs J at one of her break stations, he informed her of the impartiality required of Commonwealth officers during the caretaker period and reminded her that the office could not be seen as supporting one party over another. The offending sticker was on Commonwealth property (the tea trolley) and must be removed.

Mrs J opened her mouth as if to begin the arduous process of protest, but then thought better of it. She liked her job. Ripping the sticker from the urn she planted it across her front, declaring as she cupped and lifted her ample bosom, 'This is not government property!' The nonplussed officer, having completed his mission, had no response.

One of our clerical colleagues was Linda, who created a stir one day when she wore a blue and white checked shirt tied in a knot just above her belly button. This wasn't the usual mode of female attire at work and the broad display of flesh, combined with Linda's youthful enthusiasm, drew many admiring glances from the male community (this was the 1970s).

Mrs J happened to notice these observations and remarked, 'I was a very good-looking girl as well when I was that young.' There were a few murmurs of doubt which led Mrs J to offer to bring a photo to prove her claim. True to her word, on arrival of the next morning's tea service, she announced that she had brought the photo. Mrs J had certainly not exaggerated. The photo was of a young leggy blond with attractive features. One wag commented, 'I always like a woman in uniform, what is that you are wearing?'

'Oh,' responded Mrs J, 'that was taken when I was in the Hitler Youth.'

Mrs J had two sons, also of a physical build that reflected their mother's fine cooking abilities. She often discussed her sons, who seemed to spend an inordinate amount of time 'assisting the police with their enquiries'. Mrs J explained how she maintained a strict discipline at home and her 'boys' were invariably picked on for reasons she did not understand. She explained that they both had nice financial nest eggs as a result of her judicious management of their finances. This involved the 'boys' bringing home unopened pay envelopes and Mrs J doling out what she thought was a reasonable amount of pocket money.

With considerable distress she told us later on that the 'boys' had taken their bankbooks and cleaned out their savings for a trip to the big smoke (Sydney). She had no idea when they would return to Canberra, but Mrs J seemed more concerned about the $10 000 stripped from their accounts. We never did learn whether the 'boys' ever returned home.

Her go-to man in such circumstances was the local federal MP, Kep Enderby. Enderby was the ALP candidate elected to the House of Representatives at the by-election held in May 1970 following Jim Fraser's death. Mrs J was filled with admiration for Kep, who seemed to have the happy ability to resolve any matter she brought to his electorate office on Ainslie Avenue.

And so it was that, following Whitlam's victory in 1972, Enderby was handed a somewhat poisoned chalice – he became the first Minister for the Capital Territory. Mrs J was delighted; her man was now in government and his increased influence would surely be to her advantage.

The machinery of government changes post-election saw the demise of the Department of the Interior: responsibilities were allocated to the new Department of Services and Property under Minister Fred Daly, while some of us were now staff of the Department of the Capital Territory.

Minister Enderby called his first meeting of his senior departmental officers shortly after his elevation to the Ministry. Gathered in the ninth-floor conference room of Electricity House, they heard with undoubted pleasure the rattle of Mrs J's trolley as she came through the door to attend upon the gathering. To the surprise of most around the table and those lesser beings seated along the walls, Mrs J almost ran the length of the room to clasp a stunned Enderby's face in her hands and plant a kiss on each cheek – declaring her everlasting admiration for his achievement.

As order prevailed and the serious business of teatime was resumed, Mrs J beamed at the Minister and asked, 'Mr K, what would you like?'

'Well,' responded Kep as he settled back into his seat, 'I would like a cup of coffee Mrs J.'

There was a microsecond of silence, then the world of Mrs J exploded.

'What? You want coffee? *I am a tea lady!* If you want coffee have your wife bring it to you!'

No Minister, particularly a recently elevated one, had ever faced such a baptism of fire. There were surreptitious glances across the conference table and the palpable expectation of an equally explosive ministerial response.

'Ahh Mrs J,' sighed the Minister with an air of resignation, demonstrating their long association, 'in that case I will just have white with one sugar.'

In my time I had two significant encounters with Mrs J. The first was a morning when I had awoken with a stiff neck and happened to mention it to Mrs J on her morning rounds. Mrs J, always helpful to a fault, was right on the case: 'Ahh – that is not a problem – I will fix for you.'

She moved around my desk to stand behind me and plunged both thumbs down between the collarbone and the neck. Tears welled in my eyes as I slapped the desktop and called time but to no avail. I was pinned in my chair by her considerable downward force. I reckoned that her thumbs were at the second joint before I felt their removal with relief. With considerable conviction Mrs J announced, 'There – now don't tell me that does not feel better!' I concluded that she had been watching Star Trek and that I had survived her two-handed version of the Vulcan nerve pinch.

The second was a consequence of the first. I was determined to square off and thought that the best way to do so would be psychological rather than physical. How wrong I was.

As tea arrived and Mrs J began pouring our measures from memory, I happened to remark (somewhat courageously I thought), 'Not more of your slop Mrs J.'

As she placed the cup on my desk, she moved remarkably quickly for such a large woman and grabbed my nose between her first and second fingers – pretty much as you would do gently with a child – but this nose grip held all the strength and fury warranted by an affront to her professional abilities. I pulled back, she did not release, reaching forward to balance herself on the desk with her free hand. At this point, the desk decided that Mrs J's weight had exceeded its design limit and collapsed. We both went to the floor, with my nose still tightly gripped.

Mrs J finally released me with the comment, 'No more tea for you, ever,' before rising to her feet with dignity. Somewhat stunned colleagues in the corridor parted silently as she resumed her tea-dispensing duties. I carried a strawberry-like nose which slowly turned a shade of purple before resuming its normal condition. I was never served another cup of tea by Mrs J.

POLES

TRACEY HAWKINS

THURSDAY

With a folder wedged under her armpit and juggling a hot cup of coffee, Carrie Whitcomb scooped up the handle of a cane basket with her free hand and pulled the door to her office closed with her foot.

'Carrie, wait up, I haven't added mine yet. I forgot to do it during the lunch break,' called Jody Rogers, slipping a small wrapped present into the pile. 'Don't you love Secret Santa? It's always good for a laugh,' she said, eyeing off a large white box topped with a red satin bow. It was balanced on top of the other wrapped presents in the basket. 'Ooh, I wonder who that's for?'

'No peeking,' said Carrie swinging the basket out of Jody's reach. Turning to her staff, Carrie nodded her head towards the empty meeting room at the end of the corridor, 'Time folks, bring your coffees, snacks … whatever, we have eighty minutes allocated to us, let's make it count.'

Settled at the oval table, Carrie laid out her files as her team took their places. The room echoed with their lighthearted banter. She smiled, it was the last team meeting for the year, and the second-last day of the working week before the office shut down for the holiday period; even Carrie felt the buzz.

Keeping an eye on the clock, Carrie summarised their last meeting and ran around the table for updates. She wasn't surprised by some of the lame excuses and misdirected blame for outstanding matters, but she made her instructions clear, 'All files need to be completed and back to me by four o'clock tomorrow – no escaping early … and no sudden sickness,' she warned. Stacking paperwork back into a folder, Carrie relaxed her mood. 'Now we have one last item for today – and that is Secret Santa.'

The group chose to start the gift exchange with Phoebe Parker, the newest member to join the department. Phoebe picked through the basket seeking the gift with her name on it. Easing back in her chair, Carrie surreptitiously watched her team, updating her mental notes on each. She did this regularly. During her years in various departments as team leader, she'd quickly learnt that effective supervision meant understanding an individual's personality and what motivates them. And that meant knowing something of their lives outside of work.

A few weeks ago, Carrie had told her team she was moving on to another position in the new year and that she'd been asked to select one of the team as a temporary replacement. Ever since the announcement, Carrie's convivial working team had turned to hell on wheels. She'd oscillated from manager to moderator as her staff vied for praise and attention. They all wanted to be in the running to fill her shoes. Conflict was commonplace.

Tomorrow, Carrie would inform the team of her decision. She knew that the person she'd selected would not be well received by some.

For weeks, she'd weathered the scrutiny – they were all on the alert. Climbing the corporate ladder came at a price. Over the years it had cost her old friends who barely called anymore knowing she'd not make the events they planned.

Worst of all it had cost her Liam.

Five years together and the plans for marriage, their future … over. Carrie had ambition, she was a high-flyer. Liam had known that from the beginning and, excepting a few rocky periods, they'd been good together. She'd been blindsided by his reaction to her last promotion. The new job had proved to be the death of their relationship.

Turns out Liam had wanted a large family and for her to be the home parent. Carrie wanted maybe one child and a career. How could Liam not get it?

Carrie was jolted back to the present by buoyant laughter. Phoebe, a twenty-something slim blond, and five minutes into her career, held high a small dog figurine with a bobbing head. Phoebe giggled as she flicked the head with a meticulously shaped red-coloured nail. Carrie groaned. Scatterbrained. Phoebe was not her type, but Carrie did remember having time for manicures, and that was a point in Phoebe's favour

Angela O'Grady, secretly known as 'Lazy Angie', greedily reached her pudgy hand into the basket for her gift. Carrie knew Angela would definitely not like the new appointment. In her mid-fifties, married and heavily overweight – Angela's moods swung like a kid's swing. She'd had ambition in her early days, so Carrie had heard, but somehow, over the years, Angela had lost her drive and passion. Maybe she'd lost her appetite for success – despite appearances. This wouldn't happen to Carrie. She was only headed upwards.

Carrie bit her lip, hiding her smile as Angela studied the book she'd unwrapped: *Happy thoughts to start your day.* Quickly, Carrie scanned the others, looking for a reaction from the giver, but found none. Well played, she thought.

As the basket slid around the table, Carrie's eyes lingered on Eileen Yates. Resentful that she was descending into her late forties divorced and raising two young boys alone, emaciated Eileen was a cliché. Bitterness and loathing were eating her alive.

Eileen's behaviour had been a growing concern for Carrie over the past five months. Guilt tempered her thoughts – Carrie hadn't really appreciated how much the divorce had impacted on Eileen until Liam had changed her own world. Delighted with the scarf she'd unwrapped, Eileen draped it around her neck as a rare smile filled her face.

'It suits you,' said Terry Byrne. Married for thirty years, and wise with his words. Terry was well accustomed to pleasing his difficult wife with the niceties one learns are expected in a troubled marriage. He'd performed a miracle and brightened Eileen's gloomy demeanour.

Terry, unlike Eileen, was a solid member of the team and ever hopeful of a promotion. He was a frequent flyer applicant for positions. Although Terry had been selected to fill in for temporary roles, he'd never been given a permanent position. He was one of the few who accepted it for whatever reason and did his job regardless of his knockbacks. Terry was duck's feet beneath still waters, thought Carrie.

'Chocolates, my favourite,' said Terry, graciously opening his gift box and passing it around the table.

Alex Martinelli swallowed a chocolate and reached into the basket. With a dramatic air, he found the small, slim parcel with his name on it, held it aloft, and smiled with perfect white teeth. Alex was gorgeous and knew it. He nodded his thanks for the boxed pen.

Alex had arrived in the department thirteen months earlier. An up-and-comer, headed for success – a handsome thirty-two-year-old Australian, born to Italian parents. With a double degree under his belt and entry into the grad program, in a few years Alex had risen through the ranks like a startled bird in flight. He would end up secretary of a department one day – Carrie had seen his type before. She saw herself in the mirror every day.

Although subtle, the quick exchange of eye contact between Alex and Phoebe didn't surprise her. She'd seen the evolutionary change in Phoebe's working wardrobe with each passing week. It had grown more striking each day, as had the whip of her head whenever Alex was near.

Alex enjoyed the boost to his ego and paid Phoebe due attention in return. Sadly, thought Carrie, try as she might, Phoebe wasn't meant for the ambitious Alex.

Alex had also been considered for Carrie's new position. He knew she'd been selected and had brushed it aside. Nothing had changed workwise. Alex dutifully adhered to his assigned jobs, but distanced himself from Carrie with social niceties. He spoke to her if needed – with a smug smile stuck permanently on his face.

Carrie watched Flynn McDonald playfully pull the basket towards him. Flynn was thirty, ruggedly good-looking, and a sharp dresser. He worked well with the team and butted heads with Alex daily. There was a rivalry between the men that provided interesting conflict; both were a match for each other. Carrie could have reigned them in, but found their competitive antics amusing. Flynn too had plans for his career progress but didn't push it like Alex. Nor did he threaten Carrie with underhand play.

Two stud bulls in the pen – and Carrie in an agreeable position to possibly open the gate for one. But, something about Flynn bothered Carrie. At times, when his emerald-green eyes looked at her – hard and cold like the stone – she felt an icy shiver down her spine for no good reason. She couldn't put her finger on it.

Flynn pulled the tie from the wrapping paper and held it against his white business shirt. 'Thanks, it matches my eyes,' he said with a smile.

'Wow,' giggled Phoebe, 'it does.'

Jody was next to select a gift. She grinned as she scooped up the white-boxed gift that had previously caught her eye. Carrie watched as Jody read the name on the card, looked back at Carrie, raised her eyebrows and replaced it. Searching through the basket, she found a large gift card with her name on it and showed great delight for the movie vouchers she found inside. Jody – affable with others, focused on work, efficient, and rising up the public service ladder, was more than capable of performing higher duties and had done so a few times through the year.

She'd been a great addition to the team a few years earlier. She always had a smile at the ready, a gorgeous-looking girl, albeit single – which Carrie couldn't understand. She'd seen Jody eyeballing the stud bulls on occasion and while both men were quick with a smile and a little flirtation – Jody had struckout as far as Carrie knew.

Carrie got along with Jody. Until recently, they'd attended the same gym four times a week after work, but were not what Carrie would describe as good friends. Jody didn't disclose much of her private life.

Carrie looked at Jody, 'Why didn't you take the mystery box? It caught your eye.'

Jody laughed, 'It has your name on it. Actually, there's two presents in there – both yours.'

Picking the boxed gift from the basket, Carrie was surprised to see it did indeed have her name on it. She put it aside and reached for the smaller gift first. 'There was one Secret Santa gift each – not sure why I get two,' she lightly chided, flicking her eyes around the table. Peeling the wrapping open, Carrie couldn't help but laugh at the waterproof notepad inside.

'Brilliant. Now I can write to-do lists in the shower,' she chuckled.

'Open the other one. I can't wait any longer to see what it is,' said Jody.

Lifting the lid, Carrie was astonished to find it held a ticket.

'Oh my,' she said. The ticket was for a special exhibition at the National Gallery. 'Thank you so much.' Carrie smiled at each of her team, trying to gauge from their expressions who had given it to her. They all shrugged and shook their heads. Dismissing it as nobody wanting to claim favouritism with the boss, she let it slide.

At the loud rap of knuckles on the glass door Carrie sighed, 'Okay our time's up, back to work.'

Once settled at her desk, Carrie opened the box again. The generosity of the gift had surprised her given the difficulties she'd had with everyone over the past weeks. Taped to the inside of the lid, Carrie spied a folded note she'd not noticed before.

Meet me Friday @ the NGA

7.00 pm in front of Blue Poles

What the hell? What did it mean? She read the note again. Friday at seven. The NGA wasn't even open at that time. Was it? Closing the lid, Carrie placed the box in her carry bag. An exhibition was definitely something she would go see, but she was hardly going to turn up to a mysterious rendezvous when she didn't have a clue who that was with.

*

FRIDAY

Carrie couldn't shake the nagging mystery of the note. She'd arrived early to work, powered through the stacked files on her desk, churned through emails until finally stopping to grab a coffee midmorning. Leaning against a bench, she'd chatted to some of the team before rushing off for another meeting with heads of department.

Lunch had been a quick sandwich in her office as she signed off on the many outstanding briefs that landed in her inbox. The team had followed up as requested. Now, hidden behind her large computer screen, she took a few moments to observe the others.

Who had given her the gift? Maybe she'd find out tonight – there was an open invitation to all staff within the department to meet for Christmas drinks at Walt & Burley Bar. Why the secrecy about meeting her? Why not just ask her if she was free to meet before drinks?

As she peeped over her screen, the first to catch her eye was Terry. No. He seemed unlikely; not his thing to go to the gallery. He'd often mentioned he wasn't into art. But ... he had said he'd come for a drink tonight. And that was rare.

Flicking past Terry, she considered Phoebe. Fingers flying across the keyboard, Phoebe paused momentarily to toy with the silly nodding dog. Smiling, she picked up a page, read it and began typing again. Art and Phoebe didn't figure in the same sentence.

What about Jody? She was into arty stuff. And she'd mentioned on more than one occasion she did evening art courses at CIT.

Why wouldn't she have owned up? Carrie thought the two of them had what she considered a light friendship. But, Carrie realised, there'd been a change since she'd split from Liam.

By chance the week before, Carrie had overheard Phoebe and Jody chatting in the kitchen. Jody was telling Phoebe she had a new man in her life that kept her from the gym and that she was keeping fit in other ways. Why hadn't Jody told her she had a boyfriend? She'd mentioned to Jody that she was no longer in a relationship. Jody had been sympathetic but insisted the single life was more fun. When had that changed? Things had cooled between them. Why?

A beep from her mobile startled her.

Did you get my message?

Liam

What message? Carrie checked her phone again but there wasn't any other message from Liam. Did he mean the message in the Secret Santa gift? Why would he want to meet her at the gallery? Shit! What did he want? Maybe to get back together? Although she'd missed him in the past six weeks, nothing had changed. Unless Liam was finally seeing sense? No – unlikely. How would Liam slip the gift into the basket?

He didn't know any of her staff. Except … Jody. They'd met when Liam had come to pick Carrie up from the gym. He was waiting outside as she and Jody left the gym together and Carrie had introduced them. Since then, he'd seen Jody a few times in Carrie's presence, always after gym sessions. Liam knew they worked together but that was all. He wouldn't know how to contact Jody. No. Liam must have left the gift at reception.

Carrie put her phone aside and tried to focus on her work. She couldn't decide whether she wanted to meet Liam, so didn't reply.

Her head roiled with questions. What if Liam hadn't sent her the gift?

Again, Carrie looked out at her team working in the open-plan area. Eileen was stabbing a message out on her phone with a dagger-like finger. She was seriously unhinged, alternating between bitterness and obsession with her ex and his every move. Carrie doubted Eileen had the time to spare for art galleries, what with her kids to care for. Besides, she probably couldn't afford such a gift.

The last people to consider were sitting side by side, seemingly working harmoniously on a brief they had to finish. Had it come from one of the bulls? Changing position to ease the ache in her neck from straining, Carrie stood and walked around the room, purposefully edging her bottom on the end of the desk to give her a front-on view of the pair.

She was only in her mid-thirties, and it wasn't altogether ridiculous to consider a relationship with either. Was that it? She'd felt their admiring eyes on her and remembered the buzz. When had Liam last looked at her like that and made her feel special?

Flynn, a tad younger than her, was in the ballpark. Although he unnerved her, if she was honest, she did like the mysterious edge that came with him, and he was easy on the eye. He definitely had the confidence to surprise her with something like this.

Alex? He had the wits and charm to romance a girl into bed. But would a date at the gallery lead her to his bed? Bloody oath it would! The thought made her laugh out loud and the bulls looked her way. She waved her hand to let them know it was nothing, headed back around the table to her chair and busied herself at her desk.

She was preparing to make her announcement when the thought hit her like a bullet. Liam must have given the gift to Jody to put in the basket, that's why she'd made a fuss over it.

Jody. Liam.

Then the pieces slid into place – shit! What a bloody fool she was.

*

FRIDAY NIGHT

Carrie merged into the traffic and pushed hard to get home. It had been an awful finish to the day. Her announcement had been received with mixed responses. Some surprised her, others not at all. Jody had made a good show of her delight and surprise with the news – although Carrie had informed her she'd been successful before telling everyone else. Given the circumstances of what she had figured out, Carrie had forced a smile on her face and felt the grip in her stomach tighten.

She'd given a temporary elevation to a colleague who she believed was screwing her ex-fiancé. Feeling like the total idiot she was, she'd hurried away telling everyone she'd see them at drinks. Carrie thought she saw Jody roll her eyes and smirk. She had, hadn't she? The text from Liam said they needed to talk. To tell her what? That he was seeing Jody? The thought crippled her.

The reaction from the bulls had also left her flat. Flynn had shrugged and flashed angry green eyes. Alex stared hard with a tight mouth and had then stormed from the room; how bloody dramatic. Alex liked an exit. No doubt she'd hear their thoughts over wine tonight. Terry had been disappointed but congratulated Jody. Angela had huffed and puffed about how unfair it was. Eileen had actually snarled – Carrie had been panicked that Eileen would snap.

Meeting them again for drinks would be tough. But she would face up to it. Carrie was a leader.

She'd also decided she would meet Liam head-on. If he was her Secret Santa messenger – well, she'd be at Blue Poles and they would finish this for good.

With the clock ticking she sent Liam a message, quickly showered, then flung open her wardrobe, pushing clothes aside to find the right outfit. Something stylish. She needed to look delectable to leave Liam with a clear image of what he was missing and, on the other hand, it had to be something suitable for drinks. Tough call. Her silky red dress would be perfect. Slipping her feet into heels that showed off the shapely turn of her calves, Carrie hurried out the door.

*

Carrie gave a last glance in the mirror of her sun visor, ran her tongue across her teeth to ensure no residue of lipstick had adhered, and flicked her fingers through her hair. 'Looking good girl,' she said to her reflection, flipping the mirror closed.

Looking good – feeling like rubbish, she thought as she headed to the stairs leading from the underground carpark to the entrance of the NGA.

Inside, the NGA was quiet. A sign directed her to reception for the special gallery display. She showed her ticket at the desk and was directed to the first floor. Passing the display room, she made her way to the open gallery where she found Blue Poles.

Standing in front of the artwork, Carrie acknowledged she was not an artistic type. She struggled to make sense of it. It looked to her like a mass of spaghetti and cheese, with a top dressing of long blue slashes. Obviously, she lacked the finesse to be an art critic.

What had Pollock been thinking when he painted it? Reading the free leaflet in her hand, Carrie shook her head at its purchase price. One point three million dollars.

An NGA guard stepped up beside her. 'Excuse me, but this section is closed to the public now.'

'Sorry,' said Carrie. 'I have a ticket for the special showing,' holding out her ticket, 'but I had a message to meet someone here.'

'That sounds mysterious,' said the guard.

'It is. I don't know who my date is, but they said meet here at seven,' she said and smiled.

The man frowned before he answered, 'I guess I can wait with you for a bit, but I'm sorry, then you'll have to go.'

'Thank you so much.'

'You know it's worth three hundred and fifty million dollars today?' the guard said.

At this Carrie laughed. 'Even I could paint that badly for such money.'

The guard shared her humour. 'Me too. I didn't like it much at first, but it grows on you. I've a better appreciation of art since I started working at the gallery. I research the paintings so I understand them better.'

Carrie nodded and studied the picture again.

Glancing at her watch, she saw she'd already spent time waiting. Ten more minutes and she was leaving. Every few minutes she checked the room to ensure she didn't miss Liam – or maybe someone else. Scrabbling in her bag for her phone, Carrie shook her head in disbelief. Where was her phone? What had she done with it?

Thinking on what she'd done when she got home, she knew she'd sent a reply to Liam and … put the phone on the edge of the bath so she could hear if he sent back a message while in the shower.

'Bugger,' she snapped.

'Date stood you up?' said the guard.

'Maybe? I left my phone at home so I don't know if they've sent a message.'

She *was* expecting Liam to meet her. He wouldn't stand her up out of spite, would he? He wasn't like that. Her thoughts ran in circles. Had she got it wrong about the ticket? Maybe it *was* someone from work?

Ten minutes later Carrie figured she'd been the butt of somebody's joke. She thanked the guard and stormed from the gallery down the internal stairs back to her car.

She flipped on her lights and drove up the exit ramp into torrential rain. Peering through the slash of her wipers, she followed the road towards Kingston. Carrie soon found she had to fight to keep the car straight in her lane, so she pulled off into a side street near a small area of bushland. Reaching for her umbrella, she flipped it open and stepped out into the downpour. Her rear back left tyre was puddled in a heap. 'Fucking hell,' she cried into the night.

Walking seemed her only option. She had walked a few metres from the car when suddenly a car pulled up behind her. A flutter of alarm set her heart racing until she saw the familiar face emerge through the rain.

'Oh … it's you,' said Carrie.

'Carrie, what're you doing in the rain?'

Carrie laughed, 'I have a flat tyre and I've left my phone at home. I was headed for help.'

'That explains why you didn't answer my messages.'

'I picked the best time to forget my phone. Not!'

'Well, you're lucky I saw you. I just caught a glimpse of you in the streetlight.'

With a laugh Carrie asked, 'Hey, fancy helping me change my tyre?'

'Sure, happy to.'

Crouching down beside the wheel rim, Carrie traced her finger over the torn rubber. She leaned in closer. The tyre had been cut in strips 'Holy shit. I reckon someone's slashed my tyre. Must have been …'

The words hung on her lips as she had her last thought: … *slashed while I was at the gallery …*

*

The blow from the tyre lever shattered the left side of Carrie's head. Lying in the gutter bleeding profusely from the deep gash in her scalp, Carrie slid into a dark void. The second blow drove fragments of bone deep into her midbrain and pierced her brain stem. Carrie clung to life, sipping in air as her chest rose and fell in small puffs.

The third and final blow killed her.

CAPITAL NEWS

The stories you need, now.

Woman's Body Discovered Near Kingston Foreshore

By Ted Waterstone

December 23, 2019 – 1.20 pm

Canberra police made a horrific discovery on Friday night when the body of a young woman was found lying in a gutter near the Kingston foreshore.

Police have not released the victim's identity nor the cause of death at this time.

Detective Inspector Rick Williams, from the Criminal Investigations Team released a brief statement asking the public for help.

'We have a female victim, aged approximately in her thirties, who has been the victim of an attack that has resulted in her death. We are treating her death as a homicide and ask for any witnesses who may have been in the area of the Kingston Foreshore sometime between 8 pm and 10 pm Friday night, who may have noticed something, or know anything that will assist police with their enquiries, to please contact Crime Stoppers on 1800 333 000.'

Police investigations are continuing.

CENTENARY

PAUL DALEY

They were calling it the celebration of the century. The biggest party ever held in the city.

Marlowe still occasionally read 'The Times' – like when he came across a discarded copy on a bench or picked up a freebie at Fyshwick Markets. He still listened to 666 in the afternoons, too. If he was awake. Old habits die hard. Current affairs. Fresh food. Newer ones too: smack, shoplifting, burgs.

One of the local politicians interviewed on the radio this morning reckoned there were free buses and bands and food for the party to mark the city turning a hundred. Marlowe and Jaya had always liked a party. At least before they'd bottomed out. The gear made it hard to stay awake. And when they were awake at parties, they usually spent their time riffling through the medicine cabinet for sedatives and sussing out the kids' bedrooms for loose change. People stopped inviting them.

So they stayed in mostly. Except to score or to hustle the money to do it. Busking was one way. Jaya used to stand outside the supermarket in Manuka and play violin, the battered felt-lined case – with its 'Girls Grammar' sticker on the outside – hungrily open on the paving, waiting for the loose shrapnel of passers-by. Some knew her. Parents of girls she'd gone to school with a couple of years back and some of the kids too, would toss a few gold coins, even a note or two, into the violin case. These days she kept her eyes clenched shut when she played, so they never crossed glances.

But she felt their gazes. She knew what they thought when they looked at her, with her knotted hair and blotchy skin and dirty clothes. And then they'd see him, sitting on the bench behind her, a sketchy, spidery figure in ripped jeans and a hoodie, rolling a ciggie out of squashed fag ends he'd scraped from the footpaths. Marlowe, the bad-arse boyfriend who'd dragged her down from the time they'd met in Year 11. 'Well fuck them,' she always thought. She had no use for their sympathy. Just their money.

This love was a mystery to all but Marlowe and Jaya. Only they never needed to parse over it, about how they clung together, conjoined in pain from the past and from fighting the junk, from the constant fear of losing each other, from subsisting day-to-day to scrape together enough to kill the pain. How they rode that spiral together, way down, the sublime ascents when they held each other tight on the floor and kissed and petted each other's hair and cheeks, and the frightening descents, always like a slowmo elevator into quicksand. Always together. Together forever. That was their vow.

She'd quit busking a few months ago after he pawned the violin without asking. Now she just begged while he burgled.

*

The politician on the radio said one of the bands at the centenary party was The Church. The band liked the city, he said. The singer lived here as a kid. Marlowe had never heard that before.

The lady on the radio wondered if they'd play 'Under the Milky Way'. Marlowe knew it. His dad had loved it. He used to listen to the CD *Starfish* all the time. He'd skip the other songs and go straight to 'Milky Way', play it on repeat, 'til it drove the boys mad.

The music died after the accident. Marlowe only realised that later.

They'd fought like buggery, his mum and dad; their way of coping with grief, they said, whenever Marlowe told them to shut up. Never mind that his was to cut and tattoo and hurt himself. They didn't even notice when he carved his twin's name into his forearm with a compass.

Alex

They split when his mum moved to Melbourne with a woman she met at uni. The old man, Roger, could barely keep it together, got pensioned out of Treasury, hit the piss, stayed inside and forgot to pay Marlowe's school fees.

That's about when Marlowe and Jaya found each other. It was a Year 11 party in Turner. She came out the back to smoke. He was sitting under the apple tree drinking goon. He liked her cheekbones. She'd never seen a Grammar boy with tatts before. She liked his edge. And while they drank and smoked under the tree that first night she told him about her grandfather and how her parents never believed it. Stories, her parents called them. Stories she'd made up. As the goon took hold he talked in disjointed snippets about Alex. He told her how he dreamt all the time of what happened, how in the dream he always managed to hold onto his twin after the boat capsized but how, when he woke up, he remembered straight away that it wasn't true. The tears came as he told Jaya how Alex had drowned. How he knew he could only have saved his brother or himself – but he wished Alex had been the one to make it.

They couldn't wait to leave school and home. They found a room in the Red Hill flats – badlands in the middle of a silent suburb with big houses and pools and golden ash trees and Subarus with bicycle racks in driveways and beagles in the backyards. They'd never felt safer or more invisible, because nobody ever looked out for the poor people in this city, except when they break in.

*

Everyone will be at the birthday party, that lady and the politician said on radio. That made it the best day ever for burgs.

Marlowe reckoned Roger would be there in the park with everyone else. If anything could drag him out of the house it would be The Church.

And he also knew Rog would've been too lazy to change the combo on the safe in the bedroom, where he kept the cash and the four gold ingots he'd inherited when his old man died. Rog always said he'd give Marlowe and Alex two each on their twenty-first.

Marlowe told Jaya about the gold.

'Ali would've sold it and invested in the stock market,' Marlowe told her. 'He's the one gave a shit about the future.'

She said, 'You're alive because you're stronger. You hung onto the boat Marly and he didn't. You're a survivor.'

'Yeah.'

'The winner.'

'Yeah?'

'Yeah. And know what they say 'bout winners?'

'Inherit the earth?'

'Yeah – take all.'

'The gold?'

'Uh-huh.'

'Ali would've wanted me to have it.'

'It's yours – so take it. Go on.'

*

They crossed the bridge on the bus. The water was the kind of blue Marlowe remembered from the holiday he and Alex took to Greece with their parents when they were sixteen. It was the last family holiday. The water in the brochure was such a deep blue that he could never imagine the sea looking anything like it. But as the plane came in over Santorini the sea had looked just like it did on that tourist pamphlet.

The Captain Cook jet was on, its plume vivid white against the cloudless sky. Jaya remembered the times, as a little kid, she'd ridden her bike with training wheels along the path in front of the gallery and the High Court just over there, with her dad hovering in case she should she fall, and much later when she'd gone to the library – the Nash – to meet boys from the grammar school. None of them were anything like Marly though. Not a patch.

The bus stopped at the lights. Hundreds of people were crossing Commonwealth Avenue, making their way to the party in the gardens. They carried picnic blankets and eskies and fold-up chairs.

She laughed. He didn't see the joke.

'What's up? What's so funny?' Marlowe asked.

Jaya said, 'It's just I can't ever imagine having that sort of life, like Mum and Dad did – being organised enough to buy that stuff, to own things like that, to make a picnic ... you know?'

'You mean, to plan stuff?'

'I suppose, yeah. Something like that. I don't have anything anymore Marly.'

''Cept me.'

'Yes. That's all.'

Marlowe looked out for Roger. But he didn't see him.

They sat in Corroboree Park watching the house. It had gone to shit a fair bit since Marlowe's mum pissed off. The hedge was dying and the straw-coloured lawn was way out of control. Paint curled off the sienna-coloured verandah roof like strips of old orange peel. There was no sign of the staffy, Mandy, who'd always hung in the front yard, standing up against the gate in the low hedge, observing the street life and waiting for pats or treats from those who knew her. Kids, dogs – Roger was incapable of looking after either.

The front door slammed behind Roger. He looked like crap, with a patchy, grey beard and in jeans and an old business shirt that hung off his lanky frame. He rubbed his eyes against the glow of the afternoon.

He walked off towards the city, lit a smoke as he went.

Marlowe used his old key to get in.

They laughed as it slid into the barrel and turned.

Marlowe said, 'Slack bastard – couldn't even be fucked to change the locks.'

'Saves us busting a window but,' she said.

The house was surprisingly – like OCD – tidy and clean.

They went to the fridge, took out a plastic container of leftovers and heated it in the microwave. He instantly recognised the smell – Dad's green chicken curry – of all those Sunday night dinners in front of the TV. He took two small bottles of beer from the fridge. They sat at the kitchen table. Jaya ate voraciously. Marlowe leaned over his plate, inhaling the steamy aroma of spice and sugar and coconut milk.

They clinked bottles.

She said, 'Happy 21st babe.'

He took a swig, swallowed hard and wiped the tears from his eyes with clenched fists. His voice cracked and thinned as he said, 'Let's get the gold and get out of here.'

'Yeah,' she said. 'But first …'

She took a spoon from the drawer and started cooking up a fix.

*

They played 'Under the Milky Way' as the light faded. Roger loved that song. He stood on the lawn among the crowd and sang along and swayed and wondered if Marlowe still had the same number and if he'd pick up if he rang to say 'happy birthday' and whether he was still with that girl and even if he was still alive.

He remembered the birthday the boys had in Greece and then felt himself fall into the familiar thought that he'd let it all slip away to this since Alex. It all got lost somehow, along with Ali, in the accident. When The Church finished their set, he turned and walked up the hill. As he meandered through the mums and dads and kids sprawled on their blankets, he lit a smoke. He thought about staying. But there was no reason.

He walked into the house, fed *Starfish* into the player, forwarded it to 'Milky Way'.

He sang his way into the kitchen, froze when he saw the two beer bottles on the table, the dishes, the burnt spoon and lighter.

He went to Alex's room.

Marlowe and the girl were fast asleep on Alex's bed. She looked angelic in sleep, with her blonde hair fanned across the pillow and her skin so pale it was almost translucent. Marlowe frowned and mumbled to himself. A patina of perspiration made his forehead glow.

Roger touched his son's hair and whispered, 'Happy birthday.'

He bent forward to kiss him.

AN IDEAL CHOICE

NICHOLE OVERALL

As the military parachute floated through a cloudless sky, its khaki-clad occupant took stock of the windswept floodplain shimmering beneath him in the noonday sun.

Ringed by hills of blue to the south-west, smaller scrub-filled rises to the north, and the distant, rugged outline of the Great Dividing Range in the east, the valley that lay between was bisected by a meandering river. On either side, seemingly adrift in the pastureland, sat a few obvious testaments to public service and bureaucracy. These were interspersed with a relatively small number of modest dwellings; relative because this was the Australian capital after all, and three decades had passed since it was declared so in 1913.

Closer on the eastern flank, the paratrooper could make out the bustling borough of Queanbeyan. The more than century-old NSW township had generously – though with an eye to future benefits – relinquished 910 square miles of its hinterland for the formation of the Federal Territory; renamed the Australian Capital Territory on its twenty-fifth anniversary. He knew too, that since a time beyond imagining, this land was held close by its traditional inhabitants.

This mock invasion by the 1st Australian Parachute Battalion was a training mission and the paratrooper's first visit to the area. He had, though, studied the Canberra plan in great detail. As yet, the view didn't match the vision of its American architect, Walter Burley Griffin, or the artistic depictions provided by his equally qualified wife, Marion. Still, a scenic setting without a doubt, and deserving of the press-bequeathed sobriquet: the 'Bush Capital' – even if the phrase was sometimes employed as a slight.

The expectations for the planned national masterpiece were always going to be difficult to realise. From the outset, agreement couldn't even be reached on where it should sit and how it would be established.

That alone would take nearly ten years of bickering, boastful claims, and politicking to resolve – the final decision far from unanimously embraced. Then, one world war was followed by a second just twenty years later. In between, the greatest economic disaster of modern times unfolded. The far-reaching effects of the Depression added to wartime depletion, and saw the initial fitful work on the Commonwealth's fledgling heart come to a virtual standstill.

Even as the country limped towards recovery, realisation of a grander Canberra continued to be elusive. And that aerial perspective of the city's unfulfilled promise was to stay with him as much as the oft-bandied taunts of an 'extravagant political whim' and 'a good sheep paddock spoiled.'

*

It was 1943 when John Overall – architect, self-made man and that same paratrooper – made his unusual entrance into the capital. Canberra was bereft of almost everything that would make it deserving of such a title. Inhabitants numbered a mere 12 000; primarily those servants of the public prised from the previous bastion of government, Melbourne.

Upon Overall's return fifteen years later, and no longer wearing the uniform of a decorated Lieutenant-Colonel, he would disappointedly note that 'the "city" remained little more than the same scattered settlements I had gazed down upon … earlier.'[1]

Nonetheless, the opportunity to rectify the situation was by then firmly within the former Battalion Commanding Officer's grasp.

After Walter Burley Griffin's tenure as Federal Capital Director of Design and Construction ended in 1920 due to irreconcilable viewpoints, the Federal Capital Advisory Committee was formed to take charge.

Four years later, the Federal Capital Commission (FCC) assumed responsibility. Under the direction of engineer Sir John Butters, previously known for his involvement with the Tasmanian hydro-electric scheme, the FCC achieved a modicum of success. It could claim the graceful Albert Hall and the Renaissance-styled commercial hubs, the Sydney and Melbourne Buildings. Most significantly, it would oversee the physical statement intended to mark Canberra as the First City: Parliament House, opened to great fanfare in 1927. By 1930 though, the Commission was abolished and its activities devolved to various government departments.

Its 1938 successor, the National Capital Planning and Development Committee, would survive almost four times as long. However, as another advisory body, it appeared to exist merely to suggest the idea of progress. Oversight was next shared between two Commonwealth departments: that of the Interior (planning), and Works (building design and construction).

A lack of clear direction and its impact would be laid bare in a damning report tabled in 1955 by the Senate Select Committee formed to review the development of Canberra. Among numerous recommendations, it called for the capital's planning future to be directed by a single authority. Finding 'a powerful champion'[2] in Prime Minister Robert Menzies, two years later, the National Capital Development Commission (NCDC) was established. Overall, then forty-four, was declared 'an ideal choice' as its inaugural Commissioner.[3]

His mandate was fourfold: consolidate the city as the seat of government and an administrative centre; provide the necessary facilities; give Canberra an atmosphere and individuality worthy of a national capital; and establish it as a comfortable and dignified place to live.[4]

Over the next decade, the metamorphosis of the largely featureless plain would be as dramatic as the lack of activity that preceded it.

*

The background of John Wallace Overall, son of a Sydney publican, seemed to offer little promise for notable achievement.

Born in the same year the foundation stone was laid in Canberra, Overall was raised in the Masonic Orphan Schools in Baulkham Hills. This followed the early death of his alcoholic father and the inability of his incapacitated mother to care for him and his two sisters.

Despite these inauspicious beginnings, Overall managed to earn a place at the Sydney Technical College – the alma mater of many a prominent architect before a formal university course was offered in that city. His first commission was to build a home for his struggling family.

Overall was awarded the prestigious NSW Board of Architect's Travelling Scholarship in 1939, but, like so many other young men, career prospects were waylaid when he enlisted to serve in the war.

An engineer with the 2/13th Battalion (9th Division), Overall's mettle was just as apparent on the battlefield. He received a Military Cross and Bar for 'outstanding leadership & disregard for danger' and 'great courage, devotion & initiative'[5] at El Alamein and Tobruk. His wartime service also saw him survive a trek through the deserts of North Africa after a daring escape from a prisoner-of-war camp.

Having married Margaret Goodman in 1943, in that same year he was promoted to CO of Australia's first airborne unit. On his return to civilian life in 1946, Overall was appointed Chief Architect for the South Australian Housing Trust. Within seven years, he was elevated to Chief Government Architect in the Commonwealth Department of Works in Melbourne.

By 1958, the Overall family – then with three of an eventual four sons – had arrived in their new home. They too, were somewhat underwhelmed with a capital city that was, from their perspective, 'barely a couple of suburbs, with a rickety old bridge over a willow-clogged creek almost the only connection between them, and hardly a shop to be seen.'

Overall's first task was to hire a talented team to complement his personal, and ever-expanding, skills base. He was 'particularly obstinate'[6] about making his own appointments, wanting to find loyal professionals he could trust to get the job done. He also augmented his reputation as a consummate bureaucrat; described in a 1965 edition of *The Age* as a 'quietly dynamic man, under whose friendly charm one senses an implacable will.'[7]

This was perhaps best demonstrated by his wrangling with his political masters over the jewel in the capital crown – that central body of water around which the city continues to expand, mature and shine.

Always the centrepiece of the Griffins' design, their lake encapsulated Charles Scrivener's 1909 contour survey of the site and its waterways. Contentiously, the scale and scope of the lake had been progressively reduced, but as Overall himself told it, the matter reached near hysterical proportions with claims its construction would have dire ramifications for the city's financial, environmental and social future.

In 1959, while Prime Minister Menzies was abroad, the initial funds agreed by Cabinet to jump-start the massive project were removed from the Budget. Rather than try to convince those responsible otherwise, Overall patiently marked the days until the return of the absent PM. As the plane touched down at the Canberra Airport, the Commissioner charged with preserving the integrity of the master plan was waiting for his boss – on the very tarmac itself.

The necessary finances were promptly reintroduced. When Parliament approved the measure in 1960, and as fellow bureaucrats would attest, the very next morning Overall had bulldozers at the ready in the centre of the site.

As many as 500 workers at a time toiled, excavating to a depth of seven feet and removing thousands of tonnes of soil. Islands that would become features of the waterway were created and bridges to traverse the lake were built. The wall to dam the waters of the Molonglo River rose ever higher. Well inside the projected time frame of four years, filling commenced. An inopportune period of seven months without a drop of rain did little to assist, but finally the dry spell broke. The dusty remains of a golf course and racetrack, and skeletons of makeshift abodes, disappeared forever, and the critics fell silent.

Artificial and ornamental perhaps, but no less beautiful for it, Lake Burley Griffin was officially welcomed and embraced by the city on 17 October 1964. For his perseverance and professional intractability – and numerous other services to the flourishing capital of the nation – the unpretentious child of a barman shortly afterwards became Sir John Overall.

*

During Sir John's more than fourteen years at the helm of the NCDC, Canberra grew from a population of some 40 000, to home for almost 165 000. The authority he steered oversaw the creation of buildings and institutions of national significance – now Australian icons – and largely held true to the original aesthetic of the capital's designers. Almost six decades on from its official naming, Canberra was finally coming of age, transforming into the Cinderella of the Griffins' imaginings: 'a city not like any other city in the world ... an ideal city.'[8]

'An observer of its progress for all [his] adult years'[9], Sir John Overall's commitment to the Territory he'd helped shape continued unabated, and would do so until the end of his life in 2001 at the age of 86.

In 1972, he was invited to chair the jury that would choose the 'positive, dominant' High Court with its distinctive 'wall of glass and cascading water feature.'[10] Five years after moving on from the NCDC, in 1977, he was nominated as Chairman of Assessors to select the design for the greatest national architectural initiative since the Sydney Opera House: Australia's next Parliament House. He then served on the Parliament House Construction Authority, working closely with winning principal architect, Romaldo Giurgola. Sir John considered the last two roles among his most significant.

Over a period of thirty years, these achievements and advancements did more than just mould a city; they cemented it as a place worthy of the mantle of national capital, one which looked to enshrine the traditions of, and provide a beacon of identity for, all Australians.[11] They ensured it was elevated beyond politics. It was also Sir John's firm belief that, as the 21st century approached, there beckoned 'a wonderful opportunity to finally establish Canberra as one of the great National Capitals.'[12]

*

Mount Ainslie was named for James Ainslie, overseer of Duntroon, one of the early landholdings on what Europeans christened the Limestone Plains. Local legend held that the Scotsman died and was buried on its slopes after being thrown from his horse – and that his ghost could be heard there still. It is also believed he fathered a daughter, Ju.nin.mingo – potentially the first child in the area born to a white settler and an Aboriginal woman.[13] Subsequent research revealed that in 1835, a decade after his arrival in the Colony, Ainslie returned to his birthplace. Imprisoned for various offences there, his life ended ingloriously when he committed suicide nine years later.[14]

The 163-metre rise that bears his surname is an important one, defining the northernmost land axis point of the Griffins' design. Described in Walter's notes as one of the 'top galleries' of the 'irregular amphitheatre', it also provides the most expansive view of the much-changed city that lies beyond.

Almost directly beneath, the Australian War Memorial (1941) faces out to Old Parliament House which sits in front of the new House, completed in 1988 – the bicentenary of European Australia and the seventy-fifth anniversary of its capital. These opposite ends of the heart of the original plan are separated by the lake – without which 'Canberra would have been a failure.'[15] The artfully balanced landscape is adorned with easily identifiable cultural monuments. In all directions, original and newer suburbs radiate, and visible in the distance, the surrounding regions to which it owed its genesis.

At the summit of Mount Ainslie there is a bronze memorial plaque for Sir John Overall. It is a generous acknowledgement of the life's work of a dedicated public servant. From humble origins to more aspirational heights, much of his journey mirrored that of the city to which he devoted his efforts. Fittingly, the milestone of the capital's centenary in 2013 would also have marked the hundredth birthday of the man to whom 'much of the credit for the remarkable development of Canberra is due.'[16]

---

1 Overall, J. *Canberra: yesterday today & tomorrow: a personal memoir*, The Federal Capital Press of Australia Pty Ltd, Fyshwick, 1995, p. 3.

2 ibid., p. 29.

3 'Works architect as Commissioner', *Canberra Times*, 30 January 1958, p. 1.

4 National Archives of Australia, *Research guides: government records about the Australian Capital Territory*, Part 1, Chapter 5.2 <http://guides.naa.gov.au/records-about-act/part1/chapter5/5.2.aspx>.

5 *Honours and Awards (Recommendation): John Wallace Overall*. Military Cross, 30.12.1941 <https://www.awm.gov.au/collection/R1578918>; Bar to Military Cross, 5.11.1942 <https://www.awm.gov.au/collection/R1578917>.

6 Overall, op. cit., p. 41.

7 'The Canberra plan', *The Age*, 27 February 1965, p. 2.

8 'American designs splendid new capital for Australia', *New York Times*, 2 June 1912, p. M3.

9 Overall, op. cit., p. xvii.

10 ibid., p. 99.

11 ibid., p. 167.

12 ibid., p. 159.

13 Hall School Museum and Heritage Centre, *Rediscovering Ginninderra: Ju Nin Mingo*, <https://museum.hall.act.au/display/1939/person/2191/ju-nin-mingo.html>.

14 Henderson, J. 'James Ainslie: stranger than fiction', *Journal of the Royal Australian Historical Society*, Vol. 98, Part 2, Dec 2012, pp. 227–248.

15 Overall, op. cit., p. 54.

16 Uren, T. (Minister for Urban and Regional Development), *Retirement of Sir John Overall*, press release, Parliament House, Canberra, 13 July 1973.

THE HISTORIAN'S CONTRACT

CARINA MERRITT

'It's a gorgeous view.'

'It is.'

They sat together on the Mount Ainslie lookout. It was a cold Canberra winter night, and no humans dared to be out in this bitter wind. Lights shone from the War Memorial, Questacon, Parliament House. Lake Burley Griffin was black, and you could see the wind hit the water angrily, stirring it up into a frenzy.

'I've lived in many large cities. It's so strange to see one that was laid out from the very beginning.'

'The map-makers were our kind,' Algernon said with a smile.

Baeth looked across at him in surprise. How had she missed this in her research?

'But, aren't we forbidden to interfere directly with humankind?'

'Yes, we are. Those two were quite the formidable pair, however.'

'So, it wasn't on your watch?'

'No, I only came here in the fifties.'

'I can't believe you've been in one place for so long.'

Algernon laughed.

'Canberra does that. It sucks you in, and suddenly decades later you realise you stayed.'

'But it's Canberra. Most expect to come here for work, stay for a while, then return to a more sophisticated city like Sydney or Melbourne.' Baeth was puzzled.

Algernon raised his eyebrow at the would-be Historian. Despite her impressive CV, she was so very young.

'I had my flock here. Two Mavians, One human.'

Baeth nodded in understanding. The Ba'Ret oath forbade Mavians from revealing themselves to humans, even those they loved. If Algernon or his shapeshifting children had a calling and chose to leave, their disappearance would devastate their human flock.

Love a human, hurt a human. The old children's chant ran through Baeth's mind.

'It 'd be lovely to settle down and think of a flock,' she said aloud, looking out over the city.

'The Historian position here is pretty much perfect for it.'

She looked at him sideways.

Mavians could shift into any bird species, so naturally she tried to carry some of her avian history into human shape. Her hair was bright blue, her clothes billowing – silks and wools in stained-glass colours. She retained something of her true form about her face. A small nose, thin lips and amber eyes. She had adorned her body with jewels.

He was much older and had no need for trinkets.

His sons however, did appreciate such things. Well, they could do with a fierce mate like her. She'd been a peacekeeper for two decades before applying for this position. Flitting about the world, rescuing humans and animal species alike.

'I see through you, Old Bird.'

'I never doubted that you would.'

'Are your children aware of your matchmaking intentions?'

'We breed differently to humans Baeth. We don't have their social hang-ups.'

'It is said that Historians soon find themselves emulating human social standards; it appears that you are no exception to that generalisation, Ba' Algernon.'

Algernon smiled. 'Ba' Baeth, there's little harm in meeting them.'

After a pause, Baeth continued. 'I am here for the job Algernon. A job that usually has a twenty-year term. If we don't get along, or the flock doesn't turn out, life will become … awkward.'

'Why don't I show you another view and we can discuss this when we get there?'

Baeth nodded. Even if she chose not to accept the job, it was always lovely to discover new places, and Algernon was interesting company.

They shifted. To signal respect, Algernon chose his true form which was a crow. Black as midnight, charcoal eyes and a hint of blue on the feathers on his tail. When she shifted, they looked completely out of place. Wrens and crows were not known to socialise together. Now they were no longer human, Baeth's tiny brown body looked even more minuscule next to Algernon's.

They went as the crow flies towards Black Mountain.

Baeth shivered as they flew. She wasn't used to the cold and realised if she stayed, she'd have to practice other avian forms to find one better suited to the climate. Though, when she thought about it, the Superb Fairy Wren was a species common to the area and would have adaptive qualities that would ease the sharp edges of the frigid weather. Lost in her thoughts, she wondered briefly what Algernon's children did for a living. What sort of souls they were. Baeth had heard much about Algernon, his work, his gentle nature, and intelligence. If those attributes had passed to his children, then they would make adequate mates. If she was in human form, she would have shaken her head. She was here for a job, not a mateship.

They reached Telstra Tower in no time and sat on the railing of the viewing platform which had closed to the human public at 10 pm.

Algernon shifted and Baeth took his lead.

If humans were around, they would have been more than a little surprised to see two people casually sitting on the tallest beam, swinging their legs, no apparent fear at the distance to the ground.

The young woman blended into the night, but the shock of white hair on the older black man stood out dramatically.

'So, I read the contract. It's pretty much the same as any Historian position, except for the human shifter clause.'

'Correct. A test you passed tonight with flying colours I might add.'

'Why is it there though? Human shifting takes a bit of effort.'

'Because of this city. When you do covert operations, or interfere for the greater good, you need to use a different face and shape. Everyone in Canberra knows someone you know and discretion is vital.'

'Are there more than the standard Mavian events in Canberra? I couldn't find anything about the particulars using traditional research.'

'No, only we have that information as Historian. Passed orally from one Historian to the next.'

'And you won't tell me unless I sign up?

'Of course,' Algernon replied with a smile.

'Honestly, you did a thorough job briefing me in the first part of the interview process. I can't think of many other questions to ask.'

'You came all the way out here; I assume you are at least interested in the job?'

'Of course. I wanted to see it for myself though. So many of my peers tried to dissuade me.'

Baeth looked out at the view. From this vantage point, they could see Canberra in all directions. It was quiet. She could see trees everywhere and grassland; nature and city combined, joining the best part of both worlds. Apart from how spread out it was, the city was in an ideal location.

'You are pretty young in our years. What made you think to take such a job?'

'I've always been fascinated by history. I think my experience would be well suited to this environment. I also, well … I'm pretty sure I had a calling.'

He watched her as she struggled to get the sentence out.

When their kind received a calling, it did not pay to ignore it.

'If you've had a calling, why are you fighting it?'

He knew already. Baeth was of his children's generation, and their human and Mavian notions crossed over far too much.

'Because I would like to choose my path. Not what the Ba'Gurra dictates.'

She referred to the magical stream that connected their kind.

They watched as a flock of gulls landed under the lights in the car park below.

Baeth raised her eyebrow at Algernon.

'What are they doing here so far from the sea?'

'They live inland too. But most of these are Mavian.'

'Oh seriously?'

He tried hard not to roll his eyes. It used to be back in the day that you could tell a bird from a Mavian. The young had lost that skill though. Maybe he would teach her. Perhaps she would listen.

'What do you think of the graduate program?' he asked her.

Her answers on paper had been exemplary, but a truth written on paper is different to a truth told face-to-face.

'I think it's a fantastic idea. I'd be honoured to work with you.' She hesitated, but after a deep breath continued. 'After I heard the calling, I dreamt of my mother and she repeated what she had told me all of my life. *Baeth,* she would say, *our truth must be learnt from our Elders, or else it will disappear forever.* The graduate program, well, it just felt right I guess.'

Algernon tried hard not to show a hugely satisfied smile. He had to maintain a degree of professionalism and expressing his glee would not do. Not yet anyway.

'I do have some more information about the human side of things, however.'

Algernon took a folded piece of paper out of his brown tweed suit.

'This is the human contract. Permanent part-time position with the AFP.'

Baeth looked over the contract. As she looked at it, Algernon saw disquiet play across her face. After a good twenty minutes considering the contract, she handed the piece of paper back to Algernon.

'You aren't taking it?' he asked, surprised. He had thought Baeth to be the perfect fit.

'I'm not saying no, I'd just like to give it a little bit of time to sink in. It's quite … restrictive.'

'It's excellent pay and part-time. That's a pretty good deal.'

She didn't have the words to explain why the contract looked like a trap. He was older, used to these things. Signing her life for another twenty years … well, it was one thing for the Historian position, something she'd always wanted to do. But the human cover? The review clause showed five years, but the unwritten expectation was four lots of five years. What if something went wrong and she got stuck having to do that for the next twenty years?

Algernon stopped himself from frowning. Wouldn't do to scare her off completely.

'How about I show you one last sight, and then you can give me an answer?'

She nodded and shifted. A flight might clear her head. She had come prepared to accept the job. There'd been doubts but she had hoped to squash them. Now she was filled with more doubts, but still wanted to take the job.

They flew for longer this time, over never-ending roadworks, the lake, and a large road with barely any cars on it. Eventually, they circled westward and landed on an unusual triangular building. It vaguely reminded Baeth of a section of the Opera House.

'What is this place?' she asked as they looked out over valleys and trees.

'The Arboretum. I love to take visitors here, and the coffee is excellent,' he replied with a grin.

It was a beautiful place.

'How long can I consult you for advice once the changeover occurs?'

'My wife and I plan to stay another couple of years, then travel if her health allows it.'

He paused and looked into Baeth's eyes.

'Canberra has been my home now, for many decades. My flock is here. The place means so much to me. If you were ever in crisis, you could access the mind-link, and I would be with you quickly.'

Baeth nodded, reassured. He had seemed to be that sort of soul. He was an excellent custodian for the place. Would she be able to follow in his flight path?

They chatted for a long while yet, until even fewer cars were seen and more lights flickered out. Until they saw solitary night creatures tentatively leave their homes to own the Canberra night for a few shadowy hours.

Finally, he turned and asked her.

'So, will you take it?'

She gave him an uncertain smile.

'Yes, I would love to.'

ELEMENTARY ANIMAL PSYCHOLOGY

JEFF BROWNRIGG

Vale Roxie (2001–2018)

'It's depression. Griffin has depression.'

Our grown-up daughter Laura's words hung on the edge of tears.

'How could that be? We really look after him … food and shelter and loads of attention.'

Griffin her cat, having slunk around the end of Laura's couch, threw himself onto the carpet with the bodily equivalent of a deep sigh. Now prone and cocking one rear leg in the air, he proceeded to groom what Laura called his 'boy bits' while elegantly pointing toes and flexed claws at the ceiling, affecting disdain of a tedious world and the fussing humans who imagined themselves his masters.

Griffin's tongue combed the ginger fur of his groin, and then slipped upwards towards his right, one rear paw held aloft with all the aplomb of a primo ballerino. He did not *seem* ill, but that might be a characteristic of his ailment. The vet had pronounced him depressive, so he was transformed from a plain, marmalade-coloured cat to an animal with what Laura reported was clinical depression.

Just how that determination was made was not clear. It had to be something detected in his demeanour; some telling clue discovered in observed behaviour, surely. How else would the vet know? Clearly it was the sort of affliction that revealed itself in ideas expressed in a probing dialogue between doctor and patient, but in this case … Griffin was, like his feline fellows, a cat of no words. In the past, I had heard vets talk about the current disposition of a dog, the evidence of happiness or gloom expressed in a tilt of the head or a slouch of the shoulders, the confident or half-hearted carriage of an oscillating tail.

It was not the first time I had encountered animal psychology. And relative to an earlier incident, Griffin's diagnosis was rather tame. This significant episode happened when Laura was much younger and also involved a cat – a feral cat released into the parkland in front of our house by some heartless fiend before they headed off on Christmas holidays. That cat, not yet fully-grown, crossed the street and, with mewing entreaties to both of our children, begged for food.

'Can we give it some milk?' somebody asked.

'No! We don't want to encourage it and besides, it's a native bird killer.'

The cool, logical, firmly delivered reply was, in the mind of the parent-speaker, an end to the story.

The cat mewed again, a drawn-out, whingeing appeal to human good nature. The sound seemed calculated to imply weakness from starvation. Within it, I also detected an instinctive awareness of human foibles and frailty. This cat knew very well that, by now, we were only seeing a poor suffering creature that had bravely escaped from an inhospitable park to the safety of our home.

'We can just put out a saucer,' Laura explained. 'It's only a kitten.'

A kitten it was, but one that already understood that rolling its eyes and brushing fearlessly against small human legs would be sure to elicit sympathy.

It did. 'This kitten was probably dumped and is used to being regularly fed,' I explained. 'And it is clearly not afraid of people.'

We sat and watched the cat lap at the plate of milk for a few minutes. And then it was gone.

'Back to the park,' I said and followed this with an instruction. 'We don't want it in the house.'

'But we will feed it … a bit?' Laura asked.

For three days we did and on the fourth we found it under a bush in the back garden with a broken leg. Hit by a car, while crossing the road, we surmised, it was now incapable of returning to its predations in the park.

Gingerly gathering the little moggie into a cardboard box, we were careful not to grind bone on bone. It was cautiously carried to the vet who, smiling benignly, spoke of a specialist orthopaedic surgeon and a little time in hospital. There was no mention of feline counselling, however, just the need for a few obvious running repairs.

'They'll insert a metal pin into the leg. She'll be as right as rain in no time.'

'But she is not our cat,' I explained a little weakly, a comment that clearly had not removed the ball of survival from my court. My mind busily traversed the likely cost of all the medical services needed to get her back on her feet. The costly future I was imagining liberated a little nervous humour.

'She will continue to cross the road' I went on, 'and will almost certainly be hit by another car. Once she has four metal legs, we'll be able to drag her home from the park with a magnet!' After pausing briefly I added, 'She's really not *our* cat, mate!'

'Oh, I see,' said the vet, his smile vanishing as I plummeted in his estimation. Obviously, this wasn't the time to find even the vaguest glimmer of silliness in a cat held together with metal pins and mechanical parts.

'Well, euthanasia is an option.'

'Is that expensive?' I asked, a shade too quickly, mentally adding up the probable costs of surgery, metal parts, anaesthetic and hospitalisation. Another piercing look, his coolness barely disguised. I was, he imagined, I imagined, a mercenary bastard! Water off a duck's back could not have trickled to the floor more quickly as I smiled, sadly.

Post-traumatic stress wasn't discussed at the time, not using those words, but I felt the need to twist the knife; to restore a cheerier note. With a smirk, I asked the vet if there would be a fee for counselling after the operation, should I choose to proceed with the treatment. He had my measure, now. The question was not dignified with a reply, but I wasn't expecting one really, having been playing rhetorically for laughs.

I suspect that the vet's estimation of my humanity and compassion, my generosity and benevolence, continued in glorious, unimpeded freefall.

Once home, I explained to the children that the cat had been left with the vet, who would find her the best available home, a euphemism for what happened later that day.

Occasional requests for kittens followed as our children grew, but they were told that having a dog, Pippa, our black labrador, was enough. They could spend all their energy on attending to the needs of a single creature, and one that had no time for cats.

I'd explained to Pippa before we moved from Melbourne, that she would love Canberra's fresh air, open spaces and city's enlightened attitudes in most matters, including dog walking. I have walked and talked to family dogs in our local park for more than thirty years. Pippa died soon after we arrived in the nation's capital, leaving a gap into which our children hoped we might shoehorn a cat, but that wasn't to be. To avoid any human confusion, we hastily found a new dog.

Several years of plain sailing followed, and eventually children left to make their own homes elsewhere. Three of us lingered in Belconnen: two adults and one cattle dog, all of us needing regular exercise. It was there that the next veterinary emergency occurred, its origin in canine imagination and enthusiasm – a rather long story, but worth the telling.

Our usual daily walk followed the ribbon of asphalt winding alongside the Ginninderra Creek; a popular path for walkers, joggers, and cyclists. It was also popular with snakes that basked in full sun, absorbing the heat from black tar that soaked up and stored the sun's rays, before parcelling it out to reptiles whose cold bellies relied on this warmth to keep their blood circulating.

Roxie, the current dog-person in our house, was ten metres ahead of me sniffing clumps of tussocky grass with tremendous concentration. She was uncontactable, as she sniffed, her brain managing the mass of information fed to it through her sense of smell. She would need the equivalent of a much larger microchip in her brain for her to successfully process verbal instruction while following her nose. Suddenly she stopped, pulling back her head to better focus on the last forty centimetres of a two-metre brown snake sliding slowly to the safety of knee-high grass along the path's edge.

Roxie cocked her head slightly, and we both knew the thought that rustled through her brain. The once-vital information she had gathered though the nostrils, now suddenly and completely forgotten.

'Sticks-that-move!'

Here was a stick-that-moved, moving and ready to be retrieved.

Grabbing the tip of the shining brown tail now mostly hidden in the verge, Roxie ripped the wriggling reptile, backwards, from the safe abode of kangaroo grass, flicking the alarmed creature into the middle of the path. With no sense of imminent danger, the dog bounced around it on her toes, like a boxer shaping up for the first punch. 'Come on, come on,' she appeared to be saying to the stick, which was alert and in state of high dudgeon, unwilling to gift this agile adversary any more uncontested victories.

Sticks-that-*don't*-move are, of course, compliant, lying prostrate where they fall. But this stick rose up, resurrected by the expectation that it would soon be dog-bitten. Standing with a third of its length off the ground, head facing the slavering foe, the snake swayed uneasily never taking its eyes off the corybantic canine. Roxie, ducking and weaving, wore an expression of utter delight with her circumstances. A first strike missed as she skipped sideways away, with grace once seen in the Borovansky Ballet or in the nifty footwork of Baryshnikov.

Snake eyes and dog eyes held each other with an absolute concentration. This precluded information, especially firm, spoken direction, arriving though any other of Roxie's canine senses. This was the game of chase, the instinctive hunt, driven from the deepest wells of dogdom.

It might start as a game, but would end in a kill, one way or another.

Urgent action required.

'Roxie!' I yelled. 'No!' but the command fell on deaf ears as she dodged three or four lunges.

My brain, busily assessing the situation, saw a couple of clear possibilities. Any distraction I created might result in Roxie losing focus, rendering her more vulnerable.

Words would not do.

Neither was stepping in to separate the combatants. That would probably result in me being bitten by the snake, though I was fairly confident that Roxie would allow me to drag her out of harm's way.

The snake swayed like a cobra mesmerised by the movement of a pipe-playing snake handler. Roxie bobbed about, sometimes close, but mostly out of reach. Then I saw the snake appear to hit her once, maybe twice, on the shoulder or ribs. This encounter had to be stopped.

Deciding to risk snakebite, I grabbed Roxie's collar and dragged her away several metres to the safety of open ground mowed by Parks and Gardens. We sat there while the snake lowered itself onto the path and slid away, with almost-casual reptilian aplomb, to resume its journey.

Roxie seemed okay at first, but soon developed a slight stagger.

We hurried home and I drove her to the vet. I could confidently report that the snake was an eastern brown, quite common in our park and seen somewhere along the creek almost every day in summer.

'She seems fine at the moment,' the kindly vet opined. 'But we will keep her in hospital to test her clotting times and observe her for the rest of the day. If she gets worse, we will need to give her an injection of antivenom and possibly a second. They are seven hundred dollars each, so it's best to be sure they are needed.'

Though this was the same clinic we used for annual injections and sporadic injuries, this vet was not the one who had observed my former heartlessness in the matter of feral cats.

Neither could this vet have guessed my thoughts. Roxie, now an entrenched part of my family, would, of course, have all the treatment she required, but the words ringing in my head were 'Labrador. Free to a good home.'

We had seen an ad in the *Canberra Times*.

There was, as far as I could tell, no labrador in her but lashings of kelpie, blue heeler and, perhaps, border collie. She was principally a cattle dog, genes that contributed to chasing sticks, rounding-up sheep, chooks or anything that moved. And she listened intently, with ears pricked, an action that caused wags to suggest that there was smidgen of fruit bat in her parentage.

Mind you, I also wondered but didn't ask, how much does it cost to keep a cattle dog under observation in an animal hospital? There was, however, no alternative.

I recall the suggestion being made that Roxie might have been 'a bit lucky'.

'She was probably barely touched through the thick fur of the shoulder. If it had bitten her on the lip or nose, she'd probably be dead by now. No?' I nodded. 'We will keep her in for the moment. You will need to take her home when the practice closes at five-thirty. We'll ring you if there is anything to report or if we need to inject her with antivenom.'

At the end of the day the vet rang and asked us to take her home. She was doing well, but we should watch her closely, he instructed, and if there was any deterioration take her to the all-night vet hospital across town.

Roxie came home.

After a cursory look at her dinner, surely evidence that she was no labrador, she flopped into her basket in front of the television, relaxed and restless at the same time.

About 8 pm she asked to go outside. We understood the signs and opened the back door.

Once in the fresh air she became very unsteady and, after a few shallow coughs, she deposited a small amount of bloody sputum on the paving near the gully trap. That was evidence enough. We were soon on our way to the all-night vet in Braddon.

The vet had adapted an ordinary house to a clinic. The lounge was the waiting room. Later, I saw that the kitchen was admirably suited to use as a surgery. A kitchen table had been replaced with something that looked more medical. Nearby benches were covered with jars and equipment. But first, we were asked to wait while the duty vet dealt with the patient before us. Roxie was lethargic but had not coughed during the twenty-minute car journey or since arrival.

The only other customer in the sparsely furnished waiting room was a man sitting quietly opposite us, his eyes closed, chin cupped wearily in his hands.

Roxie leaned disconsolately against my leg, panting heavily, dripping spots of bright, clear saliva on the floor. She gave no hint of being in pain.

We waited for ten minutes. A cool, palpable silence in the room soaked up the noises of the summer night outside, heavy with dust and the city's vitality.

Then the surgery door opened and a distressed woman emerged. She fell on the man's shoulder as he rose to comfort her. He was probably her husband, though he might have been a friend. There were floods of tears, but once calmed, she looked him in the eye and explained.

'He's anorexic!' she blurted before resuming her sobbing.

Anorexic!

What kind of creature might be consciously starving itself, presumably to achieve the svelte figure that current fashion dictated? Or was it some portly dachshund who mindful of his weight, cholesterol and all that German sausage, was keen to do something about it? Or could it be the couple's child, dominated by social media and convinced that his or her physical appearance was undesirable? If so, what on earth was their child doing here in a vet's clinic?

What could possibly land a dog or a cat or a goldfish in such a state?

Roxie stirred to watch the unfolding drama.

My silent questions were quickly answered.

The vet appeared from the surgery carrying a cage containing an ordinary-looking budgerigar. Maybe this was a bulimic bird that furtively vomited the day's fodder once the cage was covered for the night? Was he keen to avoid detection and, as a result, suffered the consequences or, was he naturally inclined to be slenderer than his fellows?

In one of those moments when the mind gallops after explanations, I asked myself how ordinary physiological issues might be winkled from the minds of animals? Why was this not a tummy upset? Could it not be the new birdseed from foreign parts, tainted with a chemical residue that made the budgie appear forlorn, or lose weight, or put him off his tucker?

Most important was the question of how much common language is required to adequately communicate deep, personal unhappiness?

My thoughts were soaring into previously unexplored regions.

How was the diagnosis made? What were the signs? What feelings were we humans inflicting on our four-footed and feathered friends? Laura had used the word 'depression' and now there was 'anorexia', but I suspected that the words of the treating vets had been filtered through the understanding of each pet's owner.

I searched for something cheerful to say, or, if not overly cheerful, then a few words that were faintly amusing. There had to be a pun that would work a treat.

'When did you first notice he was … seedy?' I asked in a disingenuous tone.

No reply, and after settling the bill the three of them departed, bird gently swinging in its cage, woman gently patting red eyes.

Somehow, I detected the words 'smart arse' hanging silently and invisibly in the air-conditioned waiting room.

We sat silently again, Roxie panting and dripping, her head tightly pressed against my left knee.

Within a minute or so, two well-groomed young men appeared with a real labrador.

In domestic parlance, it had a wonky rear end (as this breed sometimes does) and stood by one its masters, who was seated where the budgie-man had waited.

The dog was clearly uncomfortable with the place, though there were no obvious threats beyond unfamiliarity. It buried its head in the security of its owner's lap and was given gentle, affectionate, patted reassurance.

Perhaps it was us; a portly doggyphile and a lethargic cattle dog.

But Roxie was watching with interest, perked by the presence of another four-legged animal. Being socially well-adjusted, she stood and shuffled unsteadily across the room. Standing a little way off, she did what any self-respecting dog always does; she sniffed the bum of the labrador in a completely orthodox manner.

I suppose it was bad luck. It was certainly badly timed curiosity, but Roxie could not have known the usual fate of inquisitive cats.

The labrador suddenly and unexpectedly suffered an explosive attack of diarrhoea.

The effect of the slight tickling of whiskers about the anal sphincter might have caused the cataclysm, but like many other matters of animal health, we will probably never know. Roxie, however, through no fault of her own, was covered from the tip of her nose along the entire length of her body with a foul-smelling, half-digested, tsunami of red, dried dog food.

Roxie was having a bad day.

Lucky that the clinic had once been somebody's house. I headed for its domestic bathroom and found odd remnants of its former occupants in cupboards, plus a good supply of paper towel. I looked for Shampooch but located only a few drops of oily fluid in an old bottle of Schwarzkopf ('for dry, colour-affected hair', the label declared); not enough to overpower the stench or eradicate all of Roxie's offensive burden.

With patience, warm water, and elbow grease, I could clean away most of the mess, while reassuring her that with the hair along her spine standing up and drawn into peaks, she looked rather like an expensive Rhodesian ridgeback. I had no mental image of what a ridgeback *actually* looked like, but neither did my dog. She listened with patient attention as I massaged the little bit of Schwarzkopf into her back, pulling the hair along her spine up into spikes all the way to the base of her tail, where fleas generally hid.

As I did, Roxie looked deeply into my eyes to say wordlessly, 'This is not why we are here … is it?' It was a look at once weak, vulnerable and imploring, suggestive of a psychological awareness that was almost human. A recognition of danger and discomfort to self.

After blotting most of the water from her coat with paper towel, an operation that destroyed any vestige of her ridgeback styling, we returned to the waiting room to discover the vet there with a mop and bucket.

The labrador and his owners had vanished.

The overnight vet was businesslike and thorough. We were ushered into the surgery. Roxie was lifted onto a kitchen bench where roasted joints were once lavishly basted and where soufflés, having risen in the nearby oven, were first admired before being delivered to the dining room. Perhaps there was a skerrick of leftover meat, lingering as a sticky residue between the Laminex top and the aluminium edging of the bench.

Roxie gave it a cursory sniff before losing interest.

'She might need the injections, but we won't know until they are necessary. She can stay here overnight, and, in the morning you can pick her up and return to the day hospital she visited yesterday. We'll call if there is any change.'

Much of that we already knew.

Roxie was escorted to a cage where she conveyed helplessness and disappointment with eyes and drooping mouth. I made my cheerful, encouraging farewells at the door and returned home where, at about 3 am, a phone call woke us.

'She's a bit worse. Did you say that we have your permission to give her the antivenom?'

I felt sure that I had already cleared the way for this, but we sleepily gave permission, again.

As it happened, the injections were not needed.

I drove back into the city at 6.45 am, cool air belying the hot Canberra day that would surely follow. I was sleep-deprived, but anxious to collect my dog before the overnight clinic closed.

As the city stirred, we ambled back to the first vet where a little more observation was undertaken and Roxie returned to us – apparently recovering though not ready to walk in the park just yet.

I continue to muse on the idea that animals have feelings that can lead to psychological disturbance. I suppose it must follow, given the evolutionary closeness of all of animal-kind. I gave my dogs instruction and instructions. Was the anorexic budgie's cage a prison that caused trauma? Had elements of his treatment at home made Griffin the cat depressed? Or was it that he had somehow figured out that he was *only* a cat?

There seems little doubt that animals have feelings and that they complete complex intellectual processes, usually to please their master. By offering complete freedom to caged birds and unencumbered access to food (for example) could we so please budgerigars or moggies that they tweet and purr, deeply contented? Or are we imposing on dumb and not so dumb animals a capability that we imagine they possess? To extend human comprehension to our pets using the tools of Freudian, Jungian or other analysis is unfortunate. Creating conditions that underpin the very survival of the creatures that live with us and ensuring their comfort and care are, however, clearly our responsibility.

Roxie now stays on the lead for summer walks and concern for Griffin the cat's welfare has, thankfully, moved from his brain to his kidneys.

SECOND CHANCE

AMANDA MCLEOD

The shadows deepened across the Brindabellas as the sun set, a golden orb changing the faded landscape into a dappled mosaic. The eastern grey kangaroo stretched, scratched, and shook off the fog of sleep. Her pouch heaved and squirmed, and the joey's head emerged, eyes blinking in the late afternoon sunlight. His mother gave a him a cursory inspection and, finding his condition to be satisfactory, she moved slowly away from the stand of trees she'd been concealed in, and began foraging.

The winter had been long and dry, leaving a sparse pasture of thin, stringy grass. The doe eased along, forepaws picking through meagre stalks, nibbling when she discovered something worth eating. But pickings were slim, and she knew that, as night fell, the mob would need to forage further afield in order to stave off hunger. One joey was all she could support; already her body had frozen the development of the new life growing inside her, suspending its animation until the hills were lush again. But rain never came on the evening breezes. Each day they rested beneath a brilliant blue sky, and any wisps of cloud that passed overhead always amounted to nothing.

Slowly the kangaroos began to move off down the hills, towards open pastures dotted with livestock. As they approached the farms, food became more plentiful. The mob spread out in the twilight, heads down, jaws working furiously as they grazed intently on the succulent grass. The joey was temporarily evicted from the pouch as his mother cleaned it; he played at eating, mimicking the adult kangaroos around him as he honed his skills. He soon tired however, and was pleased to be welcomed back into the warm, clean pouch.

Night fell, and under cover of darkness the mob grew more active. They spilled down the gentle slope, taking on sustenance, the younger ones frolicking and playfully boxing each other. At the edge of the mob, the doe alternated between grooming her joey and grazing. Then, from the hills, came a bang.

The mob rose as one, heads turned towards the sound. A second bang and a third followed in quick succession. The foreign sound echoed across the paddocks, reverberating off the mountains. The mob moved suddenly, bounding away down the hills towards the hard river that snaked across the land. As they bore down on it, twin beams of light came hurtling along, accompanied by a dull roar. Most of the mob checked and turned away, but the joey's mother was young and closest to the lights. The mob's fear, the strange sounds and the dazzling lights in her eyes – all confused her and she bounded forward.

*

Claudia and David spent the evening at a winery, indulging in decadent food and wine, and leaving their stomachs full and their belts tight. They laughed heartily with their friends as they meandered out to the car park, hugging and making rash promises like 'we really must do this more often', and other such things people say in these situations.

David slung an arm around Claudia's shoulder as they approached their car.

'Had fun then, Claud?' he said, smiling down at her.

'Far too much fun!' she replied. 'Actually, far too much of everything! Far too much food, *far* too much wine, and too much laughter!' At that, she dissolved into another fit of giggles.

'Good thing I'm driving then,' he replied with a wry grin. Claudia always got carried away on nights like this.

'Abso*lute*ly,' she responded with a broad grin as he held open the passenger door. She half-sat, half-fell into her seat and fumbled with her seatbelt.

'You're in for a nasty headache in the morning,' David said as he settled into the driver's seat and started the engine.

'It'll be worth it,' Claudia said as she let her head fall back against the headrest. 'Home, James, and don't spare the horses.'

'As you wish, madam,' said David, turning out of the drive and accelerating swiftly up the road.

The black SUV hurtled through the night. Claudia fiddled with the stereo and soon pop music flooded the cabin. Claudia sang along raucously and urged David to join her. The car's headlights illuminated the road before them like daylight.

'It's lovely, isn't it, that we can live in town but be so close to the country?' said Claudia, turning off the stereo and looking out the side windows into the darkness. 'I mean, it feels like we're the only people around.' She gestured to the road before them. 'This is like a country road.'

'That's because it *is* a country road, Claud,' replied David, rolling his eyes. 'This is all farmland, and the mountains are just over there.' He waved a hand towards the Brindabellas, a black mass against the skyful of stars.

'Don't be so condescending,' said Claudia darkly. A mild headache was already setting in. She turned her head again, looking out at the shadows. Suddenly her forehead creased. 'David, what was that?'

'What was what?' asked David, eyes on the road.

'That bang. Didn't you hear it?' Claudia peered through her car window.

'Sorry, didn't hear anything,' he replied.

The second and third times, they both heard it.

'Could be a gunshot, I suppose,' David said, 'or maybe one of the farmers left a shed door open and it's banging in the wind.'

'I doubt …' began Claudia, but something moving in the corner of her eye froze the words on her lips. Then something else moved. And all at once the paddock beside the road was alive.

'David!' shrieked Claudia. 'Kangaroos!'

'It's fine, Claud,' he soothed, 'there's a fence beside the——'

The kangaroo came out of nowhere to appear in front of the SUV, and the words were ripped from David's mouth as he slammed on the brakes. A sickening thump.

David and Claudia sat in horrified silence, unable to move. The headlights lit up the horror before them, the quiet hum of the car's idling engine the only sound. Gathering himself, David turned off the engine and looked over at Claudia. She was breathing hard, eyes wide open, face wiped blank by shock.

'Claudia? You okay?'

A minute nod of the head.

'Okay, good, you're okay and I'm okay, and the car's just a car and can be fixed.' He released the breath he hadn't realised he was holding.

'David,' whispered Claudia, 'David we have to check the kangaroo.'

'I doubt it survived, sweetheart.'

'No, but what if it had a joey? There could be a joey, David. We have to check. You hit it. You *have* to go check!' Claudia's voice was rising towards hysteria.

'Calm down, Claud, calm down. I'll check, if it makes you feel better.' David hesitated. 'I don't know what to do, how to check.'

'There's a number,' Claudia scrambled for her phone, 'you can call about wildlife. I'll call them.'

*

The joey felt the collision inside the pouch. He felt the life in his mother extinguish. One small joey, alone in the darkness. He stayed still, bundled up tight. Then the pouch opened, and light flooded in like a thousand suns. Too bright, this day. The joey squeezed his eyes shut. Gentle hands lifted him from his mother's pouch and he turned his head away. The cold night air hit him and he began to struggle, but just as quickly he was tucked up again, now in a strange-smelling pouch, in the dark. There was a low hum, and other noises he didn't understand, but a warmth was rising up from beneath him and he began to relax. The hum became louder, and there was a vibration, like his mother's heartbeat. The joey's breathing steadied, and he fell asleep.

When he opened his eyes again, he was still in the strange pouch. Hunger pangs were gnawing at his insides. Was it worth the gamble to find the entrance to this pouch and look out? After a quick sniff revealed no teat to suckle on, he decided it was. As his head emerged, something touched the side of his mouth. It felt familiar even though it smelt foreign. Instinctively he opened his mouth, and it filled with a liquid that was oddly comforting. He began to suck, and the pangs abated.

'Well hello, little man, aren't you a hungry little tyke?' murmured the wildlife carer, as the joey suckled greedily. 'You seem to be in fine form, but we'll have the vet check you over in the morning. You'll need a name, though.' She sat back and watched the little joey feed.

'I know. I think I'll name you Claude, after the lovely lady who made sure you were found. I think it'll do nicely. Don't you?'

Bottle empty and belly full, Claude settled back into sleep.

BETRAYAL

SUZANNE KIRALY

My family was itinerant when I was little, so my friendships had always been fleeting. The first time I met you, we had just settled here and I instinctively knew it would be different this time. You were young and handsome, with angular features and a defined, sculptured body that was really appealing. Not only that, but you were also generous of spirit. You'd already touched many lives and I was not the only one to adore you. You were so full of dreams and filled to the brim with hopes of your own, how could I not be inspired?

As I grew older we drifted apart. You had your eye on your own future and I became distracted by other friendships. One liaison after another fed my infatuations, even though I tired of them all quickly – which should have been a warning flag, I guess. Attracted by illusions, I found little to sustain me. You, on the other hand, were more mature and steadier with all the friendships you made when I wasn't there.

I had fleeting relationships with different guys in my teens. I smile when I think of those days now. We called it 'going out', even though we never went anywhere. We fooled around in the back seats of old Zephyrs and Holden cars at the Sunlight Drive-In. But we dared not 'go all the way'. We were still fumbling teenagers, semi-grown-ups, exploring the nebulous edges of romantic encounters.

As a romantic, I think I was in love with the notion of 'falling in love'. Every relationship only lasted a few weeks then, until we each realised we had little in common. Inevitably, we pulled the plug. I think the attraction was purely physical, and so of course each liaison was doomed.

I grew older and more rebellious. I chose partners for their shock value. It was my response to being restrained 'for my own good'. Ridiculously oppressive rules filled my teenage years with angst. But that's another story.

And you? You became far more intuitive and sensible as you grew up. You planned everything to the nth degree. You were headed in a more worldly direction. I became jealous when you moved on from me and my immature ways. The crowd you hung with did not include people like me. I had become the outsider and I started to resent you as you developed more confidence. You were now debonair, with ambition and a world view of where you wanted to be. I was directionless, an immature, emotional mess. Eventually, I hated you for it.

I moved on. I didn't even give you a second thought, out of spite. My restlessness meant that I had to move away altogether. I vowed I would never come back. And deep down, I was arrogant enough to think that if I ever did, I could probably win you over again anyway … if I wanted to.

A few years later, a failed marriage under my belt, I did come back. What a surprise! You were welcoming and there were no recriminations. For that, I was grateful. I even caught a glimpse, then, of just how sophisticated you had become. But you still embraced a highly cultured society that I felt alienated from.

As time went by, I drifted, restless again. I didn't fit in and I strayed once more.

I fell for a French chef, who was married with a couple of kids. You watched from a distance. Non-judgemental. Wise beyond your years. Of course, it didn't last. He suddenly decided he wanted to leave his wife and children for me, and so I panicked at the enormity of what I had done. I was still very young and foolish. *And* I didn't love him. I had toyed with his affections, like a manipulative bitch.

Escaping overseas, I met my second husband. We married and before long, the children started coming along. We decided to raise our kids on the coast and that brought a few years of wedded bliss. While we were there, I saw news stories about you and your amazing new projects. I was not part of it all. Nostalgia came knocking at the back door. It niggled at me and I swore we'd catch up soon, but it never happened.

As time passed, my husband and I grew weary of his commute to the city for work. I felt trapped at home with the toddler and our new baby. He left for work before the children were awake and arrived home after they were in bed. We'd argue. I had no-one but the babies to talk to and they had not yet developed conversational prowess. I was left intellectually bereft. He never understood because his life had not changed. I was so frustrated and a growing resentment festered in my soul. I knew something had to give, but not before I found out that my husband had slept with a redhead at work. For hours that day, my insides clenched in fits of rage until it felt like I'd swallowed my stomach whole. Then, I remember thinking it must be karma for all of my bad choices, all the betrayals I had committed, and besides, he promised me it had meant nothing. Just an aberration. Eventually I forgave him. I did think about you then, again. A lot. But for the sake of our two children, I decided to try again.

So, we took an overseas posting and worked at putting the pieces back together. It was an idyllic lifestyle. A place where all the expats lived in the same houses, had the same furniture and there was nothing to buy and no news from the rest of the world. It was isolated and living off the grid and for a while, it was true bliss. Our relationship slowly mended. I did still write home, and sent lots of pictures, but I never got any letters back and I lost touch with you altogether.

Then one day, I heard of the bicentenary celebrations in Australia and I saw pictures of you that blew me away. How amazing you looked! You were a key figure and had a bigger following than ever; you were famous. You embraced many people and you made them all feel so special. Jealousy came knocking once more. But as I looked closely at the photos, I noticed a hint of melancholy too, almost imperceptible to others, but I saw it there. Had you missed me, perhaps? Were you waiting for me to return? Or was that wishful thinking? Why had I not appreciated what was right in front of my nose? It was you who could give me what had been so elusive in my life.

My father had always loved you. He thought you were the right choice for me. Like Egeus, he always wanted me to commit to you, and like Hermia, I was defiant. For decades I had rebelled against all that my father desired and often for good reason, but on this point he was right. I could see that now.

By the time my husband and I finally came home from the island, I had spent more than two decades thinking I'd been happy. Again, you knew it wouldn't last. You knew I would finally come running back. It was just a question of when.

Then it happened. My husband had another affair. With one of my friends this time. It was devastating. I was the last to know. Just like in the movies. But this was real life and from that moment on, it was simply a question of time. The marriage slowly unravelled, strand by painful strand; a rope untwining and untwisting, losing every bit of its previous lustre. I suffered burn marks until the rope was completely threadbare. Finally, it disintegrated. There was nothing left. It was over.

When all was said and done, and the killing fields were over, I wandered in a cloud for a while. I spent hours reflecting on what poor choices I had made throughout my life. I was no longer young and felt time trickling out. Then one morning I woke up to a news report that was brutally criticising you and accusing you of all sorts of evil. You had become a target throughout the nation. I had an overwhelming sense of rage. I felt so protective and the murky feelings crystallised.

I got the sudden urge to see you again. To be with you again. *Really* be with you. My father had been right about this; there was and would never be, no other than you in my life. If only you would take me back after all that I had done. I had no idea of how you would react. Acceptance? Rejection?

So, I came home to you, hoping upon hope, that we could be together once more. I knew if only you would take me back, this time I would never leave again. If only you could forgive the many times I had betrayed you. And most of all, if only your heart did not belong to another.

When I found the courage to see you, you made me cry. You had changed in ways unfathomable to me, but I realised how generous a soul you were. You took me back, no questions asked. I had so much pent-up emotion, I was determined to reseal the bond between us. It could never be the same bond we had when I first met you as a naive young girl, but a mature bond between the two of us, each having travelled different journeys of 'becoming'. Now we met at a new crossroads, stronger and more compatible than ever before. The stuff of enduring love and friendship. I finally had values I could be proud of; I felt I belonged.

I know you have always understood me like no other and, because you are generous to a fault, I am able to commit with all my heart to you, and only you, this time. We are one again. I am at home with you. It's where I belong. It's irrevocable. There will be no more betrayal.

I will never leave you again. I love you, Canberra.

THOSE WHOM THE GODS LOVE DIE YOUNG

JENNIFER BERESFORD

Mick dragged a stick behind him, making a winding pattern in the dry earth along the roadside. Victoria Street, in the village of Hall, was long. Gum trees lined the side of the street, cockatoos among the branches, screeching and wailing to one another while they chewed on bark and looked for grubs and seeds on the ground. Opposite were paddocks behind a long wooden fence. The snaking patterns he made with his stick carried on for quite a while before being interrupted by tussock grass as he approached Jones' Hill.

After helping his mum around the house that morning, he took a sandwich wrapped in newspaper and some milk and water in old jam jars to spend the better part of his Saturday afternoon doing what he loved most, wandering in the bush. As he wandered, he liked to watch the magpies and galahs in the tall gum trees overhead. Today he was glad to have his stick. Being September, the maggies were making their nests and he might need it to protect him if one of them chose to swoop him. Occasionally he took his younger brother Perce with him on these adventures, but he was small and tended to hold Mick up. Today he was alone with his dog, and grateful for it.

Mick could see the dust from his grandpa's threshing machine in a paddock in the distance. He could also make out the smoke from the traction engine that powered it. It was an enormous thing that made an almighty sound and the wheels of the engine were taller than the men that worked it. It was the biggest and loudest machine he'd ever seen.

The afternoon sailed by as Mick and the dog scampered about. He had seen a brown snake basking on a rock, found part of an old green bottle sticking out of the soil near the back of the cemetery and heard the bleating of sheep down in the valley of his Grandpa Gribble's farm, the Glebe, as he wandered along the ridge. If only he'd had less chores to do that morning, he thought. Had he left earlier, he might have made it to the creek and let his dog have a swim, but it was too late. The long shadow he cast told him it was time to turn for home.

Despite the hour, the sun was still warm on the back of his neck. He stopped for a moment to give the dog a drink of water from his hands, most of the water spilling onto the dry ground. Then he heard a motorcar rumbling its way down the road. There were only a few people he knew who had motorcars, including his Grandpa Gribble. Mick didn't recognise this one. He saw it pull up in front of his house next to a group of people, two of them in police uniforms, gathered outside. He began to run.

By this time of night most folk were at home, enjoying their evening meal and ready to settle in. He had been expecting to find his mother with baby Ron on her hip, stirring the dinner above the stove while his other brothers – Perce and Leo – played on the front room floor with whatever toy was in favour that day. The gathering of men outside Cooee Cottage told him this wasn't going to be the scene that greeted him today.

'Evelyn!' called one of the men on seeing Mick. Seconds later his mother sprang through the flywire front door and into the yard. Outside the front gate she knelt down and held her arms out to him. He dropped the canvas bag from his shoulder and ran into her outstretched arms, burying his face in her neck. He wasn't quite sure why, but he felt as though something awful had happened, or was about to. He breathed in his mother's powdery sweet smell and leaned back a little as she began to pull away and whisper in his ear.

'There, there, love, it's all right,' she said, 'but there's been an accident.' He placed his head on her shoulder as she smoothed the hair on the back of his head to soothe him. An image of his father leaving on his horse and dray at dawn that morning flashed through his mind. Mick held his breath. His mum's quiet voice quivered and her eyes filled with tears as she softly said, 'It's your Uncle Ernie, love.'

Tears welled in Mick's eyes but he checked himself when he saw his father emerge from the house. Behind him came Grandma Gribble, her small frame somehow supporting his plump baby brother. Through the forest of adult legs, he saw his other younger brothers, their backs leaning up against the front wall of the cottage. Perce was dangling their wooden train in front of little Leo who was trying to grab it out of his hand. Mick glanced back into the street and saw his grandpa's Ford parked along the road. He loved to ride in it, perched on the back seat, wind rushing through his hair, on his way to the Glebe. Mick was reassured to see it; Grandpa Gribble must be here too. Local men leaned on the bonnet, one wiping his brow with a handkerchief, a soft slouch hat in his other hand. Another, arms crossed and slowly shaking his head, talked to one of the constables.

His mother rose and took his hand in hers. 'Go on up to your brothers sweetheart,' she urged gently. As they approached the house his father tousled his hair with a large, rough hand. 'You right mate?' Mick nodded, looking towards his feet to avoid his dad's eyes.

The men gathered on the verandah stepped down into the garden to make way for him, all of them silent. Grandma Gribble now sat in a wooden chair near his brothers, cradling baby Ron. Mick looked up at her face, warm and firm, framed by her small round spectacles and hair greying at the temples. Then Mick looked down at the wooden slats below him avoiding her eyes too. He feared if she spoke, he would start to cry.

A familiar voice was speaking with another man inside the front door. Dr Blackall had visited Mick's mother after the birth of his baby brother and, while the adults were in the kitchen, Mick prised open the brown leather medical bag the doctor had left in the front room. The instruments and bottles he found inside were intriguing, and Mick was disappointed he didn't have time to inspect them more closely before he heard footsteps coming up the hall and had to close the bag quickly to avoid discovery.

Dr Blackall's face emerged through the flywire. 'Mrs Gribble?' he said softly. She immediately stood up, handing the baby to Mick who was sitting cross-legged next to her. Baby Ron squirmed and fussed, his body becoming stiff in his arms while his grandma moved her small, frail body towards the door and went inside.

Mick's mother approached him, took the baby from his arms and sat in the seat recently vacated by her mother. She held little Ron upright, his small, pink feet had extricated themselves from his blanket and rested on her knees. Mick looked up at her and could see she was being brave; just like she told him to be after a rousing from his dad. He placed a hand on her knee, felt the soft cotton of her floral-printed pinny under his hand and leant his head against her leg. The dog leapt up onto the porch and, as if copying him, sat down and flopped its head in Mick's lap. He felt the dog's hot breath on his leg as he stroked the wiry hair on the top of its head.

'Is Uncle Ernie gonna be all right Mum?' Mick asked quietly after a few minutes had passed.

'We dunno, love,' she whispered, 'we'll have to wait and see.' She took one hand from Ron and squeezed Mick's shoulder gently.

'What's happened to 'im?' Mick questioned as he continued to pat the dog's head.

'He got himself caught in Grandpa's traction engine, he's been hurt pretty bad love.'

All Mick could say was 'Oh' as he put his arm around the dog's neck and gave him a squeeze.

Mick was fond of Uncle Ernie. Unlike his dad, Ernie always seemed to be in a good mood. When he came up from the Glebe to visit Mick's mum, it was easy to convince him to have a hit of cricket out the back with an old tennis ball and a piece of wood. Ernie laughed a lot. In Mick's experience, grown-ups weren't all that happy most of the time, but Ernie was. Ernie was a grown-up, but Mick reckoned he couldn't be too old. He still lived at the Glebe and didn't have a family of his own like Mick's parents did.

Mick's tummy rumbled, reminding him he hadn't had his tea. Usually they'd have eaten by now, sitting around the small table in the kitchen with his father at the head, silent and tired. It had been hours since he had his corned beef sandwich. The dog, Mick thought, would be hungry too.

'Mum?' he questioned gently. 'Is there any tea tonight?' He didn't want to ask and risk making her upset, but his stomach felt so empty.

As if able to read his thoughts, his dad called out from the front gate where he was talking to the other men. 'Mick, get your brothers and follow your cousin Cedric down to the stores, mate ... they'll get you boys something to eat.'

He collected his brothers and ushered them through the front gate following his older cousin Cedric to the Southwell and Brown stores, a few hundred yards down the road. The dog came running after them and was soon ahead, nose to the ground.

At the stores Auntie Annie gave the three boys ham and cheese sandwiches on thick slices of brown bread, lemonade and cut-up apple to share. Uncle Charlie set them up on a few wooden crates outside and went back inside. Now that he knew the grown-ups weren't looking, Mick slipped his dog some of the meat from his sandwich and wiped his buttery fingers behind the knees of his trousers.

When they got back to the house it was dark and Reverend Parton had arrived, his horse and sulky tethered to the front fence. He'd come from Wattle Park, just a mile or two up the road, where his grandparents went to church. He was on the verandah, crouched down in front of Mick's mother, holding her hand in his. Her head was bowed and she was nodding, slowly. Mick's father stood a few steps away, looking on.

Mick thought about last spring, about the time baby Ron was born, when his first dog cut his back leg on the wire fence and it had gone bad. His mum had the vet come after he visited one of the farmers nearby, but he'd said there wasn't much he could do to make him better. Mick tended to the poor dog's wound as best he could but it was no use. The dog got sickly and would only eat and drink from Mick's hands. It was too hard for him to get to his bowl on the verandah. Mick woke up a few days later to find the dog had died in the night and his father had buried him out the back.

Mick had been so upset. He loved that dog; they shared so many adventures and he couldn't remember not having him around. His dad was very matter-of-fact about the dog's death and told Mick not 'to make a fuss' when he'd caught him crying about it in the days after. One day, when his dad was out working, his Grandpa Gribble helped Mick make a cross out of wood and wire and they planted it together in the ground above the patch of turned earth where the dog lay. Mick's real name was Harold but his grandpa started to call him Mick after that, because it had been the dog's name. The new name had caught on and now everyone called him Mick. Except his mum.

Reverend Parton stood up slowly, turned and nodded towards Mick's dad. As the Reverend went inside the house his mother turned, knelt down and tried to grab all three boys in an embrace. She was sobbing and now Mick's tears were impossible to stop. He figured Uncle Ernie's leg must have gone bad like the dog's.

'It's all right Mum,' he whispered, 'Mick'll look after Uncle Ernie.'

She took his small face in her hands and kissed him on the forehead. He felt the warm wetness of the tears from her cheeks against his skin.

'Yes love,' she sighed, 'I s'pose he will.'

'Those whom the Gods love die young' is the subtitle of an article in the *Queanbeyan Age and Queanbeyan Observer* celebrating the life and character of young Ernie Gribble who was buried at Hall Cemetery on Sunday, 19 September 1920.

ONE FOR THE TOAD

PHILLIP MACKENZIE

When I had checked with Jeremy about the arrangements for his dinner party, he said he hadn't noticed that I had been out of the room when he had mentioned it to the others. So, it had been just as well that I had come back from the loo in time to get some inkling of it, and, when speaking to him about something else (I forget what, now) this afternoon, I had to remind him that I'd be seeing him tonight – and to confirm with him that, in keeping with the tradition, we should each bring a bottle for the robust debate over the relative values of the various offerings.

I think I also said something, in jest, about how that ratbag Kevin Michaels would probably do his usual pompous thing and go on about everybody else's contribution, while extolling the merits of his own (but I had the feeling that Jeremy wasn't laughing).

Anyway, tonight I had brought a 2012 Pipers Brook, together with a decoy bottle of Kalimna for Michaels to ridicule; I would then produce the Pipers to show that I knew a thing or two about 'top drops'.

*

When I arrived, Sylvia seemed surprised to see me but I gave her the normal cuddle and kiss–kiss to assure her that wild horses wouldn't have dragged me away from her annual tasting-and-dinner get-together.

I must have been the last to arrive, because there was a good crowd around the tasting table and, from the aromas wafting in from the kitchen, I reckoned that dinner was about to be served – so I had timed it pretty well. I grabbed a glass and moved in to get something to taste; I had to edge past Michaels, in his scruffy corduroy suit with those leather elbow patches, his nose poking into a glass of red, sniffing deeply. He didn't even look up at me.

I put the Kalimna up front of the other bottles on the table, but took the Pipers to the kitchen, where Sylvia was fussing with something in the oven. I decided to engage her in a little conspiracy: 'Let's keep the Pipers out here for the moment, Syl, just for ourselves, and spring it when all the other stuff has dried up.' She seemed a bit puzzled, but told me there was a corkscrew in the bottom drawer. I remarked that she kept a lot of interesting things in her bottom drawer, but she seemed not to have heard me; perhaps she didn't get the joke.

I poured her a taste of the Pipers and myself a glass, and went back to the dining room, where Michaels was pouring a Hill of Grace first for himself, then for a rather nice-looking woman, who I didn't recognise. He nodded brusquely in response to my friendly 'Hello, there, Kev – haven't seen you around for a while,' and he took the woman by the elbow and guided her to the living room.

Tosser.

I finished off the Pipers and replaced it with a hefty splash of the H/G – I really can't get a grip on a wine with those mouthful tastes that Michaels and the others fuss around with. A bit pretentious, to my mind. I remember remarking to Frank and Bill, who had just come in from the living room, that the H/G was still quite young – 2011 – and they were interested to hear that I still had some of the 2005 at home.

As is our custom, Jeremy had written, on the labels, the name of the bringer of each wine, so I could see that it was Michaels, in fact, who had brought the H/G. Everyone knew that this wasn't a patch on the 2005, but it still drew a few grudging compliments around the room. I wasn't worried that Jeremy didn't get around to writing my name on the Kalimna label.

When Michaels' woman came back into the room, I introduced myself to her. She turned out to be from one of the Scandinavian embassies – Sweden or Norway, maybe Finland, I forget which – and very pleasant she was, too. Being a Nordic, she wouldn't have known much about wine, let alone Australian wine, so I explained to her that the H/G was vastly overpriced for its quality and staying power, and recommended that she stick with the Kalimna.

Leaning closer, I confided in her that I had something 'interesting' out in the kitchen which would compare well with the H/G, money-for-quality-wise, and promised I would show it to her later ... out in the kitchen.

I could tell she appreciated the innocent double entendre and, as she moved into the other room, she assured me that she would remember my offer.

Not long afterwards, Sylvia announced that the food was ready, and that we should help ourselves at the buffet. Jeremy was carving the turkey, so I offered to bring him a glass of wine but, without looking up, he declined and I got the feeling that there was a bit of tension between him and Sylvia – so I grabbed a plate and led the way around the table, judiciously selecting a bit of everything, so that Syl would know that I really appreciated her cuisine.

By the time I finished my circuit of the buffet, everyone else was on the queue – with Michaels and his Danish woman at the end. They were deeply engaged in a fairly close conversation, too engrossed to notice when I suggested that they come and join me at the table, so having claimed a place for myself, I nipped back to the wine table to grab a couple of bottles to keep me going. One of them was the H/G which Michaels had bought, and the other was a '97 Bin 707 – or was it a St Henri? I can't rightly remember now, but I noticed that it had 'Helga' on it. I now suppose that Michaels' companion du jour must have brought it.

I summoned Bill and Graham to join me to protect our interests in the bottles. Typically the senior diplomat, Bill wondered if we shouldn't leave it on the wine table so that everyone could have some. Laughing, I assured him that we were just 'looking after it', and that he couldn't expect a clog wog to be able to tell the difference between a Kalimna (of which there was still plenty in the bottle) and the Hill of Grace. On that note, we clinked glasses and addressed our dinner plates.

As I was seated at the head of the table, and they on either side of me, it was convenient for me to take charge of the bottles. Reminding them that I had arrived late and needed to catch up, I poured myself a glass of the 707 and some for Bill and Graham to taste. I suggested that they go easy on the grog, given that they might have to dodge the breath-testers on the road home. For myself, since I didn't have a family to go home to, I was pretty sure that Syl would let me doss down here for the night.

I saw Kevin Michaels hovering around the wine table, evidently looking for something in particular, so I called to him to help himself to the bottles we had with us – there wouldn't be much left if he didn't hurry. He apparently didn't hear me and, instead, found another bottle for himself before he and his Dutch woman went into the living room where, if I leaned forward a bit and twisted in my seat, I could see them performing some extraordinary contortions as they balanced plates, napkins, cutlery and wine glasses on knees and chair arms. Then I noticed Sylvia looking a bit wallflowerish at the other end of our table, so I called her to come and join us at the head of the table. She declined, rather shortly I thought, saying that 'Kevin and company' were on their own in the living room and she should join them – her experience of organising many an embassy dinner was showing.

This made room for Nancy to bring her chair up and squeeze in next to me at the head of table. She is usually a fairly boring matron, married to Frank who not long ago had retired as a half-colonel, but she can be quite jolly with a couple of glasses in her, so I poured her the last of the H/G. At this stage of the evening, she wouldn't notice the dregs.

As I was topping up my glass with the remainder of the 707, I noticed on the wine table a bottle of Leeuwin Estate. I had heard Michaels extolling the Leeuwin's virtues to all and sundry so I had to drain the 707 and get a bit of the Leeuwin before the mob got hold of it.

'Too late, Michaels old sport,' I thought, as I returned with the prize bottle to my place with Nan (who was really getting a bit pissed by now).

After dinner we got down to our traditional 'ratings game' and I was amused to hear Michaels muttering that he hadn't had an opportunity to try the Leeuwin before it was down to the lees. Interestingly, the top wine was judged to be a Passing Clouds; luckily, I'd managed get to it before it ran out. Then I had to pop out through the kitchen for a leak and what do you know – Sylvia, Jeremy, Michaels and his Lithuanian woman were getting stuck into my Pipers Brook! What a bloody hide!

As I returned from the loo, I heard Michaels saying something about 'hitting the old road'. In the living room, most of the other guests were also muttering about the gathering fog, their fear of the breathalyser (even out here in the bush), the need to get up early in the morning, and so on, and deciding that it was time to go home, but I also noticed that Michaels seemed in no hurry to leave.

What, then, had he meant by 'hitting the old road'?

By the time the other guests had left, I had settled down in front of the fire, at last, for a chat with Jeremy and Sylvia – who looked a bit weary, poor dear. So I suggested that, as soon as they had got rid of Michaels and his trophy woman, I'd help clear the place up and wash the dishes.

After a couple of delightful coffees, and a few Swiss chocolates which Michaels' woman produced, Sylvia said that she thought I might now be in a reasonable condition to get home safely if I went the long way round to avoid the breathalyser. I assured her that she needn't worry, and that I'd be perfectly happy to kip in the spare room for the night, as I had often done after their parties.

Imagine my surprise when Sylvia regretfully told me that Michaels and the German woman were, in fact, staying the night and using the bed that I often referred to, in jest, as 'mine'.

Some people can always be relied upon to impose themselves where they are not wanted and to take advantage of other people's hospitality, can't they? So I set out to 'hit the road', as I said with some irony so that Michaels could hear, and I gave Sylvia an extra-warm hug and that pat on the bottom she always likes.

*

They really should have let me stay the night – I'm not in a fit condition to be driving all this way. I could have curled up on the sofa.

'Hitting the road': in fact, now that I think of it, he had added 'Toot-toot' and they had all laughed. Hadn't I heard a couple of comments during the evening that also seemed to have something to do with Ratty, Toad, and all that lot at Toad Hall?

But, I don't know ... why should I bother about him, or her? Or any of 'em?

They don't give a stuff about me, do they? Not one of them said a damned thing about my lovely Pipers Brook.

Called me an old toad, did he? Well, we all know about jolly old Mr Toad and cars, don't we? He loved to go fast, too.

Wait up a bit – what's that damned gum tree doing in the middle of the

*

THE WATERLINE

SHERENE SUCHY

The guy striding through the glass door into the cafe caught my eye. 'I haven't seen him for a while,' I said to Monica, another writer sitting on the other side of the table. 'He's been overseas travelling in Bavaria and Transylvania. Wonder how he's adapting back to Canberra?'

The guy caught my eye and came directly to our table, leaning down to buzz my cheek with a kiss and in his familiar gravelly voice said, 'Hello luv.' I grinned and said, 'Welcome back to Canberra. How's the culture shock going?'

'What culture?' the guy said in a belligerent voice. 'There's no culture in Canberra.'

I said, 'I suppose it is a bit different to Transylvania but at least you don't have to make an effort with the language challenges!'

The guy snorted derisively and said, 'That has nothing to do with it. There is no culture in Canberra.' Finito. He dismissed Canberra as a 'cultural desert'.

He shrugged, joined a mate at another table, and sat down frowning at me. I knew his standard operating practice was to be deliberately provocative and challenging. With a career in industrial mediation, his style was combative at the best of times. Best to take it with a grain of salt.

But, I'd heard the same irritating Canberra dissing from someone in Sydney after they returned from ten weeks in Europe. No way was he coming to Canberra in 2017 to see the exhibition at the National

Museum of Australia called Songlines. He said, 'I'm into Caravaggio, not primitive art.' He defines himself through European culture, although he grew up in Asia.

I turned to my colleague and said, 'It's the Canberra lament – giving us the old heave-ho.'

Monica looked at me with a twinkle in her eye and asked, 'Is that guy always that pompous?'

'Yes.' I said, 'His "cultural tribe" is in Bavaria, not Canberra. What is culture? Monica, you're a journalist and another migrant. We've adapted to, and enjoy, Canberra culture. Interview me about culture! You know I've lived in four different countries and coached cross-cultural adjustment with expats in Sydney for fifteen years before moving to Canberra. You also know I've been an advocate for the cultural industry sector for twenty years so we know I'm biased but … Interview me!'

'Okay, what's your definition of culture?'

'Culture is a word for the "way of life" groups of people embrace that gives meaning to the way "we do things" around here. Our beliefs, behaviours, and values create a cultural identity and a feeling of belonging (or not) to a group. It's related to nationality, religion, social class, locality, and social groups with their own distinct way of "doing things". Imagine an iceberg. You see this impressive structure sticking up out of the water but the most impressive part is under the waterline … our unconscious values and beliefs, the hidden parts, drive culture.'

'What's above the waterline?' Monica asked with a grin. She knew the standard answer. We'd been to the Canberra Visitors Centre.

'Above the waterline?' I responded, 'Unsurprisingly, the amazing national institutions located here. Each institution runs the most enriching and vibrant culture programs for the public.'

'What else is above the waterline?' Monica sipped her latte and avoided eye contact with the guy and his mate who watched us from the other table. We lowered our voices.

'Well, like any city there's the cafe or coffee culture. Canberra's coffee culture evolved in response to different locales and the needs of different client groups: dog-friendly, kid-friendly, casual outdoor dining, and five-star dining where clients can post photos on Facebook. Coffee culture changes like any cultural grouping – it's not fixed. It is fluid and constantly changing – cafes open and close. This is what makes it difficult to define any culture in only one way.'

Monica looked puzzled and said, 'Surely, there's more to Canberra than coffee culture! What's *below* the waterline that really surprised you?'

I chuckled. 'We had a receptionist at a counselling clinic where I used to work who was a queen of burlesque. She was tattooed from head-to-toe and considered her body art one of her claims to fame in the Canberra burlesque culture. There's another woman who works for the public service during the day and runs a burlesque dance studio in the evenings. She has won prestigious international burlesque dance awards. That's definitely below the waterline. Then there are the tango dancers who meet weekly and do exhibition classes every year at the National Folk Festival. There's a strong classical guitar society, plus jazz and blues groups who perform weekly at the National Press Club. The Press Club is above the waterline and the music program is below the waterline. Many people don't know about Canberra's free evening music program. I've been to wonderful concerts in the lobby at the High Court, enjoyed music at The Street Theatre, and at Smith's Alternative in Civic. Go beneath the waterline. There's this completely unexpected rich performance culture happening in Canberra. What I've just described is based on what I value – other people will have discovered their own below-the-waterline cultures.'

'Wonder how many people, like that guy, think culture is just opera, symphony orchestras, and old masters?' Monica was eyeing the guy suspiciously. She then brought us back to organisations above the waterline. 'What have you discovered about the visual arts in Canberra? What about our national institutions? What do you think?'

'There are long-established, excellent, commercial and community art galleries in addition to our national institutions. Again, I have friends in Sydney who won't come to Canberra to see art at our national institutions. They look down their noses at the 'small collections' and fly off to Italy. Their choice, but a lot of interstate visitors would tell them they are missing out on some special artwork. For example, the National Museum had an exhibition in 2010 on the Canning Stock Route, with huge paintings from Aboriginal artists telling the story of the route. It was stunning. We all felt like we'd walked into a cathedral of beauty. Same in 2017 with the opening of the Songlines exhibition – you walk in and are completely immersed in the beauty and richness of Aboriginal art and storytelling. Very compelling, letting artists tell their own stories by combining ancient traditions with new digital technology.'

Monica added, 'My favourite art institution is the National Portrait Gallery. The portraits are hung at eye level so you have a conversation with the likes of Bob Brown or Fred Hollows. The text panels build on the visual conversation. They are not written in "art speak" but "plain speak".'

I continued, 'The annual Waterhouse Natural Science Art Prize at the National Archives is one of my favourite events. Surprised how many Canberra folks don't know about it.'

Then Monica said, 'Do you know anyone who has moved to Canberra in the last five years? How did they discover Canberra culture?' She was referring to a project I'd done a few years ago interviewing new arrivals from major metro centres like Melbourne or Sydney and how they adapted to the 'bush capital'.

'Well,' I reflected on a case and sipped my latte, 'their discoveries were below the waterline. There was a manager relocated from Melbourne to Canberra to take up a regional director role for a recruitment agency. He had a family and described how grateful he was for the kids because their first impression of Canberra was – not very friendly. His kids opened doors into schools, sports, and Scouts. Each organisation had its own culture, defined as "the way we do things around here". The director said his wife missed the public parks in Melbourne where she'd go play with the kids and meet other mothers. That didn't seem to happen in Canberra.'

Monica looked up from her latte and said, 'Well, if you like nature, it's a great place. Bike paths, lakes, bushwalks. Several friends go bushwalking and are part of bush repair groups on the weekends, replanting parklands like Mount Painter. It is the bush capital.'

I asked Monica about her first impression of Canberra when she moved here from London.

She said, 'I felt isolated. The suburbs didn't seem to have centres where people could go to meet in public places. Another friend moved here from New Zealand and said the same thing. She was depressed for the first year because there was no obvious "village centre" to meet people. She resolved the problem by putting the kids in childcare and going back to work. Then she got involved in an international women's development group and started a private practice. Ten years later, she has a thriving business and is a member of the Dru Yoga community. Did you know Canberra has a thriving Dru Yoga culture?'

'Okay.' I paused. 'Let's sit back and reflect on culture. *We* both discovered there's more to Canberra than meets the eye. But, why do we see it and others don't?'

Monica laughed and said, 'You don't see what you aren't looking for – or you only see what you are looking for – or you don't look at all!'

'That reminds me,' I said with an embarrassed cough, 'we've overlooked Canberra's rich literary culture. Did you know the Asia Bookroom has been operating in Canberra for thirty-plus years and is well known internationally as an antiquarian book centre? They host a monthly book group that attracts twenty regulars who read books by Asian authors about Asia – our near neighbours – that the rest of us would never know about! The National Library, local universities, the ACT Writers Centre, and Canberra Writers Festival enrich our literary culture.'

'We have only *just* peeped above and below the waterline. I wonder what we are missing?' I asked.

Monica and I turned to say thanks to the guy who prompted our conversation. He was sitting back sipping his coffee, with his cravat wrapped at a jaunty angle, as he spoke German to his mate.

We smiled … a beautifully dressed, white-haired pompous man, looking relaxed and very at-home with Canberra culture.

LOCAL HAUNTS

MARG WADE

Steve slammed the ute door shut and started unloading his gear. He'd worked here many times before and loved this building, but he always felt uneasy when working here alone. Especially at night. And today his work partner, and best mate Todd, was out of town on family business so Steve was by himself. He had to find the fault and get the air conditioning running again asap. And before dark.

Steve had worked on many of Canberra's national attractions over the years. He and some of his mates had experienced weird happenings that they couldn't really explain. Tradies were great at embellishing a good tale, and the ghost stories they shared and joked about during smoko unsettled Steve – even though he knew that ghosts don't exist. Well of course not. But then the security guards at Old Parliament House wouldn't go alone to certain parts of the building at night … and there was that story of the telephonist in the old East Block in 1950 who went upstairs to get a new headset. What was her name again? She was a friend of Steve's mum – that's right, it was Ellen – who saw a girl wearing an old-fashioned bustled dress and ribbon in her hair. And the cleaner in 1966, poor thing, she was so traumatised at seeing the same girl that she ended up in hospital, never to work at East Block again.

There was Chifley's ghost at the Hotel Kurrajong too. Why would the former Prime Minister, who died at the hotel in 1951, always appear dressed in a grey suit and pointing towards Old Parliament House? Maybe he had unfinished business there, or really did want to attend the ball held in King's Hall the night he died. It is strange that many hotel guests who've seen him don't know who Chifley was, let alone that he died in the hotel, yet when they tell staff what they've seen, all their stories match. Some history buffs and lovers of ghost stories pay extra to stay in Chifley's room, Steve mused. Not for him; the thought sent an involuntary shiver down his spine.

Steve had a good idea of what the air conditioning fault might be as he headed, toolbox in hand, towards the plant room. Typically, a heatwave like the last few days will tip the balance in these old buildings. 'Heat can tip the balance of what goes on in your head too,' thought Steve. He chuckled to himself at the thought of Canberra going troppo in this heat; ironic that one of the reasons for siting the nation's capital here was the belief that, because the air was cold, men would think clearly. Yeah right.

Fortunately, not everyone was back at work after the Christmas break, so only a skeleton staff at the National Film and Sound Archive would be roasting today in the building. Steve shrugged, public servants spend most of their time having coffee breaks anyway. The overhanging trees in the courtyard cast welcome shade as he unlocked the plant room and went inside.

'I really like the eccentric design of this building,' thought Steve, as he stripped the equipment, looking for the fault. A bit of a history buff, he loved showing his visitors around the city and sharing its quirky stories. 'Canberra is so much more than the tired clichés of politicians and roundabouts,' he'd tell them.

'This place was originally built to house the Institute of Anatomy in 1930,' he'd recount. 'The institute's founder, Colin MacKenzie, was an orthopaedic surgeon who collected animal specimens for his anatomical research. He was fascinated by how koalas moved their arms. His research helped him treat people with paralysis and those injured in the First World War. He donated lots of his personal collection to the institute, including bizarre objects like fetuses in bottles, giraffe skeletons and even a soldier's foot in formaldehyde. Ned Kelly's death mask was kept here too.'

But there was a darker side to this building that spooked Steve. Like the things people saw during regular ghost tours of the dark sloping passageways in the basement. Once when working down there he'd felt a chilled whoosh of air as though someone had just walked past, but there was no-one else around. It creeped him out when he learned that the Institute was the young city's first morgue. Human skulls and body parts had lined its metal-shelved walls. Hmm. It had held the body of a murdered woman known as the 'Pyjama Girl'. Found near Albury in 1934, her identity still remains a mystery.

And then more recently, a bloke called Dan McMath and a team of paranormal investigators from Ghost Hunters of South Coast and Territories – or GHOST (of course) came up from the coast to stay the night. They used technology throughout the building to detect if anything was there. Steve wasn't too sure if GHOST was taking people for a ride, but they reported seeing a shadow move, and recorded some very strange audio of odd clicking sounds just near where Ned Kelly's skull had been kept. The thing was, the team could only hear the clicking sounds through their digital recorders. Without their headphones, they heard nothing. Maybe there was a problem with the equipment, Steve reasoned. But then he recalled the interview on local ABC radio with McMath the next morning, claiming that he was pretty certain the building was haunted.

There you had it. 'It's a fact,' Steve thought, 'this building has spooks, and not the ASIO types.'

Julia, an old schoolfriend, headed up the events team at the Archive. Because Steve was interested, she had told him a few stories of strange noises and happenings at night when staff worked late; many declaring they wouldn't stay late on their own again – they'd rather take their work home. When he'd pushed for more detail, Julia was reluctant to say any more. Steve often felt she knew more than she let on.

Suddenly, Steve sensed a presence behind him and he quickly spun around to check. What the——! … Nothing.

'Stop it,' he thought. 'I'm just jumpy because I'm thinking about all this stuff.'

Steve was getting hungry and the job was proving to be more problematic than he had first thought. 'Bugger, I'll be here later than I'd hoped. Bugger.' He decided to duck over to Maccas in Civic for a Big Mac and fries before getting stuck into the next phase of his repairs, and hopefully he could still be out before dark. When he returned thirty minutes later, the building cast a lonely shadow. Behind it, the sun was slipping low in the summer sky, generating glorious hues of yellow, pink and orange.

*

Steve's work was done. He'd sorted the problem by about 10 pm, packed up his tools and got ready to go. 'I'll come back in the morning just to check the air con is functioning properly,' he told himself.

A nice cold beer was beckoning and he was looking forward to ducking into his usual haunt, King O'Malley's, for a quick one on his way home. The plant room was noisy and to his surprise, as he emerged to leave for the pub, he discovered an event in full swing in the building's courtyard.

'God,' he thought. 'This is flash. Must be a thirties party. Fundraiser maybe?' Women were elegantly dressed in satin floor-length backless gowns with sweeping flared hems. Some topped with feather boas. Beautifully tailored tuxedos, with peak lapels and square-shouldered jackets seemed the order of the day for the men, all looking most refined. 'Appropriate,' thought Steve, 'I bet the Archive holds film footage of this sort of thing.' The epitome of sophistication!

A jazz band was pumping out a big band sound and the evening looked so much fun. Couples displayed the fancy footwork of the tango and foxtrot – 'How cool is that,' Steve thought as he turned away and strode out.

Outside the building were dozens of vintage cars. 'Geez they've gone for the whole shebang tonight,' he thought. 'Julia's excelled herself.'

*

Next morning, Steve was just about to slide out of the driver's seat of his ute when he heard a familiar voice. 'Good morning buddy, how are you?'

'Hey, Julia, great to see you.'

'I hope you've sorted that air con out for us today, it was awful here yesterday.'

'Yes, worked late last night to get it right for you guys,' Steve said with a grin. 'Hey, amazing event last night, well done, you should be pretty pleased with that one – I've never seen a party so authentic before.'

'Sorry?'

'The party – the amazing costumes, the music, dance and even the cars – it was so cool. I'd love to be part of a big do like that.'

Julia's face paled. 'There … was no event here … last night …' she stammered.

'Yeah there was, it was sensational.'

'No mate, nothing was scheduled for last night …' She paused. 'I've gotta go, I'm late for a meeting.'

Julia sped off. 'She looked like she'd seen a ghost,' and as he thought it, Steve felt intense unease rise from the pit of his stomach.

'I need a coffee,' he muttered. Steve headed into the building but, on impulse, instead of turning left towards the cafe, he made a beeline for the courtyard, the scene of last night's festivities. It looked just the same as it had yesterday and the day before, and the day before that – a bit tired, the grass burned and dry from the recent heat. There was no sign of where the band had been, no stacked tables and chairs, no wear and tear on the grass as evidence of the dance floor where the sensationally dressed partygoers had strutted their moves in front of the big band.

Steve felt sick and desperate. Fear heaved from his toes to the top of his head to engulf him. He spun around to leave, to escape, when something on the sunbaked grass caught his eye. A white feather. From a boa.

SWIMMING

MARGARET HENDERSON

Evi and the boys dumped their backpacks on the bench at the shady spot under the SUPERVISE CHILDREN sign at Manuka Pool. For a few moments the boys were like octopuses pulling off bike helmets, wriggling out of sweaty shirts and shaking off shoes. They went to the other side of the pool and jumped in.

Evi slipped off her shoes, slid her feet into flip-flops, put on her sunglasses and adjusted her scarf. She scanned the pool. The boys were at the '5 feet' mark, kicking up a foamy volcano. They yelled back, 'Hey Evi' and then kicked harder to make a bigger, frothier volcano.

There was now familiarity to this routine. Evi was settling into this afternoon rhythm. A heatwave had lingered for ten days at the end of February and going to the pool had become welcome relief.

On the first day at the pool, Evi had found it difficult. She knew no-one. The boys seemed to know everyone. Beside the lapping topaz, within the yellow walls of the 1930s pool, Evi had felt different from everyone else, awkward and exposed. As the days passed, Evi studied the patterns and codes of the pool. She chose the shade not the sun. She sat with the mothers. She bought along a book to avoid unwanted company.

Just as Evi and the boys arrived each day, the well-organised French family was leaving. One child always trailed behind. 'Dépêche-toi. Nous quittons.' Politely, people kept their eyes on the pool, but their ears were tuned intently to the family's conversation.

Three little girls in sparkly pink swimsuits claimed the sunny, shallow end. The girls seemed fused together; screaming, diving and rising as one, spouting water, mouths gaping for air.

A tall, slender young man sat nearby. He rubbed his skin with frangipani-scented cream. The fragrance reminded Evi of home on the south Java coast. Greased and oiled, he slid into one of the roped-off lanes, waited patiently for the other swimmers to turn before he pushed off from the edge with a soft kick and long arches of his arms.

The cranky old man came every day at 4.15 pm. As soon as his goggles were glued to his face, he was off racing down his lane, mouth open on one side, sucking in the air as he charged along. Ten lanes done, he sat for a few minutes in the sun to dry off. He watched the lane swimmers, never glancing at anyone else. When his mood had sufficiently returned to crankiness, he would flick his towel over his shoulder and disappear into the shadows of the portico, leaving only the trace of his wet, squeaking thongs.

A red-haired mother gently held the hands of her red-haired child learning to walk. The child squealed as it stepped in the puddles of warm water at the edge of the pool. The three girls surfaced. They looked at the little child who smiled at these rose-sparklers in the afternoon light. The girls gulped great gasps of air and submerged.

The wind tugged at Evi's scarf. She was hot. She sweated in her long sleeves and slacks. The boys swam to the pool edge below her. They splashed her. Wet face. Wet hands. Wet legs. Wonderful.

'Be good,' Evi yelled to the boys. 'We are very good!' shouted the eldest before both dived sending huge sploshes to soak Evi again.

A woman in a blue swimsuit stood up beside Evi. The woman seemed strong, confident. She smiled – or was she really squinting? The breeze ruffled her sun-bleached hair and the sun warmed her bare shoulders. 'Are they your boys?' she asked. This was the first time someone had spoken directly to Evi at the pool and her heart jumped in her chest. This wasn't the ordered world of family or university. This was the wide world, perhaps a wild world, unpredictable and encroaching.

Evi's thoughts started to melt in a gibberish of English and Bahasa. Before Evi could speak, the woman had asked another question. 'Why don't you go for a swim?'

Evi was still preparing a perfect English answer to the first question. Then she spluttered, 'I can't swim, I don't swim, I mean …'

'Well, those boys really love the water,' said the woman as she tucked her hair into an iridescent blue bathing cap and waded down the steps into the water.

Evi felt her confidence evaporate. The hot wind circled the pool. The pines leaned in, accusing her.

Evi retreated to her book. *Gardens of the Alhambra.* She looked around the pool thinking how she might redesign it – a fountain here, stonework there. As she imagined, Evi travelled, and as she travelled, the lemon walls transformed to lustrous, luscious foliage and the pool from pale blue to emerald green. Evi took a deep breath of humid tropical air and listened to the pelting of monsoon rain.

As the pool returned from green to blue, Evi saw a shape in the water sweep around the little girls and coil around the boys. The woman in the blue swimsuit surfaced and then submerged. Long, flowing, sweeping, slow. Then there was a powerful slap and a silvery flash under the surface. Evi looked hard to make sense of it. Dolphin or shark? Friend or foe? It is difficult to be sure even when the water is clear.

The wind flipped the pages of the book. Evi saw her mother lose her grip on a little boy in savage, sucking waves. Foam. Confusion. Force. Shock. A little hand locked by love and then … lost.

Evi's mother had taken to searching the sea for her little boy. She scoured rockpools and beaches. Inconsolable, she disguised herself as a fisherman, left her family and went to sea to hunt down the sea spirits who had stolen her boy. Evi believed this wave of anguish would swallow her alive like it had gobbled up her mother.

'The name's Grace by the way. Better get back to work or they'll be sending a search party.' The woman in the blue swimsuit was beside Evi, wiping herself in a thick towel. But Evi was still coming to the surface. She hadn't been watching the boys. Where were they? Her eyes dashed around the pool.

A shriek pierced the noise. Evi ran down to the shallow end steps, almost slipping. The boys – where were they? Anxiety made her blind, stupid, and mad too, like her mother.

The three little girls had formed a pyramid on the boys' shoulders. The girls were now plunging one by one into the pool. Splashes jumped and tumbled around the boys. Nobody noticed Evi's panic.

The afternoon shadows had crept across the water. Time to go. The red-haired mother smiled at Evi as she wheeled her sleeping child in its stroller to the entrance. The three little girls had changed back into school uniforms. Evi looked for Grace. She turned back to the pool and watched as the wind moved across the water. The blue shape swept by, under the surface. Evi looked harder. Nothing. Perhaps it was just one of the lane swimmers pushing off against the edge, strong and so sure of themselves.

Evi felt uncertain. The wave of anxiety was building up again. She was tired, tired of being like this, tired of being on the edge of losing self-control.

The boys loitered at the entrance with the other children hoping for ice creams. The hot wind twirled the postcard stand. A flash of iridescent blue on the cards caught Evi's eye. 'Swim like a mermaid. Lessons starting soon.' Another gust of wind sent the stand twirling impatiently. Evi took a card.

Her anxiety subsided. Evi had stayed afloat. She slipped the card into her pocket. In this strange, imperfect place, Evi resolved to learn to swim.

A LOVE LETTER TO CANBERRA, I COULD HAVE HAD NO BETTER MUSE

PAUL DALEY

After more than twenty years living, loving and writing in Canberra, I spent my final night as I did my first.

This is the last night when Canberra will be my permanent home. I've spent it as I did my first, back in late 1993, alone in the same modest motel in the inner south (park anywhere, dinner until 8.30, free newspapers and checkout at 10 am, sharp). There was bad stuff going on from a war I'd just visited, my personal life was a shambles and the only thing keeping me in journalism was the city I'd just arrived in.

Running? Not exactly. Staying? A year at best, 'til I could escape some stuff. Building another life here never occurred to me.

The last two decades and a bit is improbable history for me. I hated the city at first. It gave me reason to. The retired public servant in the flat downstairs (he wore chinos and an ironed polo shirt to tend his modest garden) complained when I left the packing boxes on the verandah for a few weeks and after every time I flushed the dunny.

Eventually the body corporate sent me a formal letter of complaint about the untidy state of my flat's externals (this will amuse many; I'm the neatest, most ordered person they know).

'Fuck Canberra,' I said to everyone.

Then I got into the work, back when a newspaper was going to be printed every day and forever and you could turn off after you'd filed a story daily (or in my case, weekly) and do other stuff, like exercise and cook and meet people. I met someone and of course it all changed and it became the best place in the country to be a journalist if you wanted bang for buck. And, yes, if you wanted to make a difference, which of course I did (want to, that is).

Like so many people in Canberra with kids, I was seduced. It is a great lifestyle, with ridiculously short front door to school / childcare drop-off possibilities. But that's not really enough reason to stay if your work is meaningless or you're isolated and lonely or among the city's invisible but numerous poor. I never noticed, because I was in Parliament House (or often overseas), how desperately quiet were the streets.

I only noticed this (and so much else about the city) when I became a self-employed, full-time writer in January 2008. I wrote my first book at a desk facing a broad window looking out on a street named after a famous exploratory ship; all the streets in my vicinity have nomenclature of famous explorers or ships: La Perouse, Arnhem, Beagle, Endeavour. How lonely, I realised, it must be for some, in these isolated places, in these big houses quarantined by bush corridors, who have no families and jobs they dislike. The vast bush around us here echoes loneliness or love, inspiration or desperation. It's not an idyll for all, though it has, mostly, been for me.

I've felt the isolation too, though – longed to leave my door, like I did in London and Melbourne, and be part of a life on the street right there. A folly, I'd tell myself, then, for everything else this place gives me.

And that's the thing here. You embrace the bush and the communities that revolve around it, or you don't ever quite connect. Like the poor. I've often thought that this city – with its vast middle class (there are few super-rich or landed types here, like in Sydney, Perth, Melbourne and Adelaide) – is a terrible place to be poor. The rest of the county assumes there is no underclass here.

But the rough sleepers – in those bush corridors and in the streets – and the beggars are everywhere. It saddens me that the public housing estate close to my house, soon to be razed, will make pitifully little allowance for social housing, under a Labor government. It pleases me, however, that, in too many other ways to name here, my city – and the Australian Capital Territory – is the most socially progressive place to live in the country.

There is a pounding heart and a warm, generous soul in this city. Communities thrive almost in spite of the serene suburbia. Artists of all sorts riff off the difference, the uniqueness of living and making life and love in a capital that is small, spread out and held in contempt by the rest of the country.

I get it. Completely. I could have had no better muse than Canberra, where intellectual life is deep and wide, where people look out to the country and the world, where the memory of the nation – incarnate in its institutions like the National Library of Australia and the Museum of Australian Democracy – is everyday.

It's misunderstood, even within the city itself. The marketers will say this is the city of Walt Griffin and Marion Mahony Griffin. That's a fallacy. You can see the ghostly visage of their geometric dream from atop Mount Ainslie or Red Hill. But the dream died with the Anglophile planners who bastardised their blueprint and superimposed a vast, sprawling suburbia for too few people on top of it.

I love it here (not in the motel, but the city). I've called it an accidental miracle of a city. Because it thrives when the planners and two world wars almost killed it, and ironically, now, because it grows in the shape Walt and Marion had envisaged, with greater inner-urban density, with cutting-edge architecture and well-planned communal spaces.

It's a great place to be a writer, although I've learnt 'Canberra writer' can be something of a pejorative. And I don't need the OECD tell me it's one of the best places in the world to live.

I'm grateful to have spent twenty-something unlikely years here in Canberra. I'll take away more than I've given, including a family, for which I'm lucky and so very thankful. And half-a-dozen books and a million or so words of journalism. Or does their home remain here?

And then there's the motel. I'm in the same room as I was in 1993. Nothing's changed. But me in the mirror.

And there's still no fucking minibar.

Goodbye Canberra.

Thanks.

Originally published in *The Guardian: Australia edition,* 23 Dec 2016.

AUTHOR BIOS

Craig Cormick

Craig is an award-winning Canberra author and science communicator. He has published over thirty books of fiction, nonfiction and children's fiction, with both small and mainstream publishers, in Australia and overseas. Much of his work deals with reinterpretations of history. His writing awards include a Queensland Premier's Award, ACT Book of the Year Award, the Tasmania Writers' Prize and a Victorian Community History Award. Craig is a former chair of the ACT Writers Centre and has taught creative writing at university and in schools, and is a great believer that good writing comes from good editing, drafting and rewriting.

Hon Dr Andrew Leigh MP

Andrew Leigh is the Federal Member for Fenner. Before being elected in 2010, he was an ANU professor of economics. He holds a PhD from Harvard, is a Fellow of the Australian Academy of Social Sciences, and is a past recipient of the Economic Society of Australia's Young Economist Award. His last book was *Randomistas,* and his new one is *Innovation + Equality* (with Joshua Gans). A keen marathon runner, Andrew hosts a podcast titled *The Good Life: Andrew Leigh in Conversation*. Andrew and his wife Gweneth are have three sons – Sebastian, Theodore and Zachary.

Ben Gray

Ben Gray recently rekindled his interest in fiction writing after learning about the Capital Culture writing project on ABC local radio. 'Eastlake and stable' is his first published piece of writing, and he is slowly working up the courage to finish writing his first novel. He enjoys coffee, bushwalking, and travel and has a keen interest in the New South Wales railways. As with many in government employment, Ben has moved on from Canberra for the time being and now lives with his brilliant wife Vanessa and their dog in the Blue Mountains, west of Sydney.

Tim the Yowie Man

A proud Canberraphile, Tim has published over one million words on life in and around Canberra. He writes a weekly column in *The Canberra Times* that explores the ACT region's natural, cultural and social history and for the last twenty-five years has hosted a range of tours that shine the spotlight on Canberra's secrets.

Simon Bryant

Simon Bryant grew up on a farm, a soldier settler block in the south-east of South Australia. After graduating with an English literature degree from Adelaide University, he has pursued a number of paths including farming, managing a radio station, working in tourism, and most recently, an extended spell in the public service in Canberra. Now retired, he is dedicating his time to a lifelong interest in creative writing and, in particular, to writing historical Australian fiction.

Jenny Morris

Jenny Morris is a regional author. She has published two children's books. Her first, *The Thing on Mount Spring,* won the UK-based International Rubery Book Illustrated Children's Award 2018 and was a winner in the USA Royal Dragonfly and Purple Dragonfly Awards. Her second book *Hare 'n' There* was also a winner in the Royal Dragonfly and Purple Dragonfly Awards. www.jennymorris.com.au

Irma Gold

Irma Gold is an award-winning author and editor. Her short fiction has been widely published in anthologies and literary journals like *Meanjin, Westerly, Island, Award Winning Australian Writing* and *Review of Australian Fiction*. Irma's short fiction collection, *Two Steps Forward,* was shortlisted for, or won, a number of awards, and her debut novel will be published in 2021. She is also the author of three children's books, with two more forthcoming, *Where the Heart Is* (EK Books) and *Seree's Story* (Walker Books). She is Convener of Editing at the University of Canberra and Ambassador for the ACT Chief Minister's Reading Challenge. irmagold.com or @Irma_Gold

Marion Halligan AM

Marion Halligan has published more than twenty books: some eleven novels – many you have probably heard of. She has been short-listed for most of the prizes on offer, and has won. She has regularly reviewed books, and likes to write essays. She has received an AM for her services to literature. *Valley of Grace* (Allen & Unwin, March 2009) won the ACT Book of the Year and was long-listed for the IMPAC Prize.

Brian Franklin

Brian Franklin was born at Tumut NSW in 1942, growing up on a cattle and sheep holding at Argalong near Tumut, the mountain forestry camp at Bulls Head on the western ACT border and later the forestry settlement at Uriarra. Over the years, as an observer (and regular participant) of the frailties of human nature, Brian has created an eclectic collection of stories, cartoons and poetry which reflected upon a wide range of passing interests and circumstances. 'The last tea lady' is one of those stories. Brian was also a recipient of the Chief Minister's 50 years Canberra Gold Award this year.

Tracey Hawkins

Tracey Hawkins is the author of children's books, novels, and adult works. Before life as an author, Tracey was a police officer with the Australian Federal Police in Canberra. Tracey's early writing career began as a crime-writing consultant and columnist while she wrote children's stories. Her two writing worlds collided perfectly when she was asked by a school librarian if she would write a 'nice' murder mystery for children. Tracey is Ambassador for the ACT Chief Minister's Reading Challenge, a Forensic Enrichment Speaker, and recently released her new picture book *Leaping Lola* in London, UK.

Paul Daley

Paul Daley is a Sydney-based author, journalist, essayist, short-story writer and playwright. He has published six nonfiction and fiction books, several of which have been shortlisted in Australian literary awards including the Nib, the Prime Minister's Prize for Australian History, and ACT Book of the Year. His journalism has been recognised with numerous prizes including two Walkley Awards for Coverage of Indigenous Affairs and Investigative Reporting, two Kennedy Awards, and the National Press Club Award for Federal Parliamentary Press Gallery Journalist of the Year. His essays appear regularly in *Meanjin* and *Griffith Review*. They have also been published in compilations including *The Best Australian Science Writing* (2016) and *The Honest History Book* (2017). He co-wrote the two critically acclaimed *Hansard Monologues* political plays and he writes Postcolonial, a column for *The Guardian* about Australian national identity, history and Indigenous culture. Allen & Unwin is publishing his second novel, *Jesustown*.

Nichole Overall

Nichole Overall is an award-winning author, freelance writer, social historian, and communications consultant. A former journalist with a BA in Communications (UC), Nichole has spent thirty years in the field, writing both nonfiction and fiction, across a variety of genres. Her 2013 book, *Queanbeyan – City of Champions*, researched and written over five years, is a demonstration of her passion for the capital region. Nichole's next project is a creative nonfiction work on a WWI volunteer stretcher-bearer from Cooma, the only soldier ever awarded four Military Medals.

Carina Merritt

Carina has published several short stories. She is working on several novels in the science fiction and fantasy genres. Carina has Bachelors of Teaching and Arts. She currently works as a high school teacher. She likes to spend time with her husband and their two children and various pets and can usually be found reading, costuming, gaming, taking photos or writing. More details can be found at: www.facebook.com/carinamerrittauthor/.

Dr Jeff Brownrigg

For most of his working life, Jeff conducted research at Australia's National Film and Sound Archive. His books, articles and lectures include biographies about Australian popular and high art performers. He was the National Wandering Historian for the Centenary of Federation encouraging 300 communities to recover and share their stories. He writes and talks about poetry. In 2010, he was made Canberra and region's Communicator of the Year. Jeff is an Adjunct Senior Research Fellow at ANU and Professor of Cultural Heritage Studies at UC. He wrote a PhD at the University of York, with supervision in music, English and philosophy.

Amanda McLeod

Amanda McLeod is a fiction and poetry writer, and the managing editor of Animal Heart Press. A Pushcart Prize nominee, her words can be found in many places, both in print and online; and in 2018 she won both the Marjorie Graber-McInnis Short Story Award and the August round of the Australian Writers' Centre Furious Fiction competition. When she's not immersed in all things literary, she's usually out with her dogs or looking for the perfect quiet spot. Visit her website: amandamcleodwrites.com.

Suzanne Kiraly

As a writer, publisher, editor, bookseller and teacher, Suzanne has over twenty years of experience in all facets of the publishing industry. As a book coach she's worked with talented Australian writers and taught them how to self-publish and make a passive income for themselves online. She runs writing courses / workshops / literary events and her greatest claim to fame is that she can recognise writing talent in others.

Jennifer Beresford

Jennifer Beresford is a seventh-generation descendant of a number of pioneering families in the Canberra region including the Southwells, Gribbles and O'Briens. Her interest in the region's history began as a child while listening to her grandparents recount stories of her ancestors. Over a number of years she has collected a library of local historical texts which provides inspiration for her writing. A former Commonwealth public servant, Jennifer currently lives in Washington DC with her husband and nine-year-old daughter.

Phillip Mackenzie

WA-born, Perth-raised, Canberra-matured, Phillip Mackenzie has previously won awards for two of his short stories. In semiretirement he divides his time between the literary and theatrical worlds, and is currently working to bring the two together – by reviewing local theatre as a member of the Canberra Critics Circle, and adapting 'One for the Toad' to the stage.

Dr Sherene Suchy

Dr Sherene Suchy is a Canberra-based social worker, educator, researcher, and writer. A nonfiction writer, Sherene has a specific interest in social action research – the value of lived experience. Previous publications include texts such as *Leading with Passion: Change Management in the 21st-Century Museum* (2004), journal articles, and chapters in books. Recent indie publications include *Keepsakes: Memoir on the 'Museum of You' & Estate Planning* (2016) and *Bamboozled: Trek Guide for Clients & Experts in Medicine* (2018).

Marg Wade

Passionate Canberran, Marg Wade, has been marketing and promoting Canberra for decades. Tired of the old clichés of politicians and roundabouts, Marg published *Canberra Secrets* (1999, 2003 and 2018), guidebooks for residents and visitors, highlighting fabulous things to see, do, explore and experience in Canberra. She seeks out things behind the scenes – the quirky, the gems, the 'secrets'. A logical extension to these invaluable guidebooks was to establish Canberra Secrets Personalised Tours in 2017, providing high-quality experiences for locals and tourists. From a teaching and communications background, Marg has worked in marketing roles in private and public sectors. You will often hear her sharing Canberra secrets on ABC, 2CC and 2CA.

Margaret Ann Henderson

Margaret Henderson's published work includes short fiction, poetry and travel writing. To learn more about writing, and to have fun, Margaret has participated in Canberra's Flash Fiction Fun Weekends, studied screenwriting at the Australian Film Television and Radio School, and immersed herself in *Poetry in America*'s online course. She holds a BA from the University of Queensland and has Masters degrees in Public Policy and Applied Anthropology from the Australian National University. Margaret lives in Canberra and in the summer she swims at Manuka Pool.

David Schembri

David Schembri is an author, artist, genre poet and designer from rural Victoria. He is the author of the horror collections, *Unearthly Fables* (in collaboration with The Writing Show, 2013) and the Australian Shadows Awards-nominated collection, *Beneath The Ferny Tree* (Close-Up Books, 2018). David's graphic design has graced the covers and internal pages of many publications, spanning a career of over 25 years. He also enjoys developing his love for comic illustration and design. Visit his website at: davidschembri.net

PLEASE LEAVE A REVIEW

If you enjoyed the stories in this book, I hope you'll take a few minutes to write a review under it on Amazon.com.au and/or goodreads.com. Books depend on reviews to spread the word and the authors in the book will be most grateful to you if you do spend a few moments reviewing this book in its entirety or individual stories within it.

Thank you in advance for your generosity.

If you want to share anything in relation to this book please don't hesitate to email me:

suzanne@suzannekiraly.com.au